PAUL

FORRESTAL

MUSHROOMS
&
TRUFFLES

A
GOURMET'S
BOOK OF

MUSHROOMS & TRUFFLES

JACQUI HURST
&
LYN RUTHERFORD

Photographed by
JACQUI HURST

a Salamander book

Published by Salamander Books Limited
LONDON • NEW YORK

Published 1991 by Salamander Books Ltd,
129-137 York Way, London N7 9LG

This book was created by Merehurst Limited
Ferry House, 51/57 Lacy Road, Putney, London SW15 1PR

©1991 Salamander Books Ltd

ISBN 0 86101 436 7

Distributed by Hodder and Stoughton Services,
P.O. Box 6, Mill Road, Dunton Green,
Sevenoaks, Kent TN13 2XX

Commissioned and Directed by Merehurst Limited
Managing Editor: Janet Illsley
Photographer: Jacqui Hurst
Designer: Sue Storey
Home Economist: Lyn Rutherford
Editor: Maureen Callis
Typeset by Angel Graphics
Colour separation by Kentscan, England
Printed in Belgium by Proost International Book Production, Turnhout

ACKNOWLEDGEMENTS

The authors would like to thank the following for their help and
advice: Ted Green, Roger Phillips, Jeff, Jenny and Ruth Stone, for their
enormous help in collecting and identifying mushrooms; Peter
Cracknell and David Livesey, for allowing visits to their mushroom farms;
Jaqui Gibson, David Robertson and Sue Baker for help with photography,
cooking and recipe testing.

COMPANION VOLUMES OF INTEREST:
A Gourmet's Book of HERBS & SPICES
A Gourmet's Book of CHEESE
A Gourmet's Book of FRUIT
A Gourmet's Book of VEGETABLES
A Gourmet's Book of CHOCOLATE
A Gourmet's Book of TEA & COFFEE
A Gourmet's Book of SHELLFISH
A Gourmet's Book of DRIED FRUIT & NUTS

Contents

GENERAL NOTES

For identification of edible mushrooms, this book must be used
in conjunction with an authoritative field guide which shows inedible
species too.

Mushroom photographs in the text section are life size except where
otherwise stated.

NOTES FOR RECIPE USERS

Quantities are given in metric, imperial and Australian cups.
Use one set of measures only; they are not interchangeable.

All spoon measures are level: 1 tablespoon = 15 ml spoon;
1 teaspoon = 5 ml spoon.

Use fresh herbs unless otherwise suggested.

All recipes use fresh, cleaned mushrooms unless otherwise indicated.

Australian users, note spring onions are the variety commonly termed 'green
shallots' or simply 'shallots' in Australia. Where a recipe specifies shallot, use
a 'brown shallot'.

Introduction

N owadays it is possible to buy quite a selection of wild mushrooms. Over recent years, high-class greengrocers and supermarkets have started selling ceps, chanterelles, horn of plenty, oyster mushrooms, hedgehog fungus and sometimes truffles, when in season. But it is far more fun foraging for your own – and there is the added bonus that they are free!

Many people shudder at the thought of eating wild fungi. This is a pity because there are delicious species to be found growing in woods, fields and gardens.

The aim of this book is to encourage you to go foraging for edible mushrooms. Here you will learn where and when to look for fungi, what to look for, and how to go about preparing and storing your find. If you are nervous about gathering your own wild fungi, at least try and buy some wild varieties to appreciate their flavours.

Finally, the selection of recipes offers original ideas for delicious soups, starters, main courses, salads and accompaniments – using cultivated mushrooms and wild varieties.

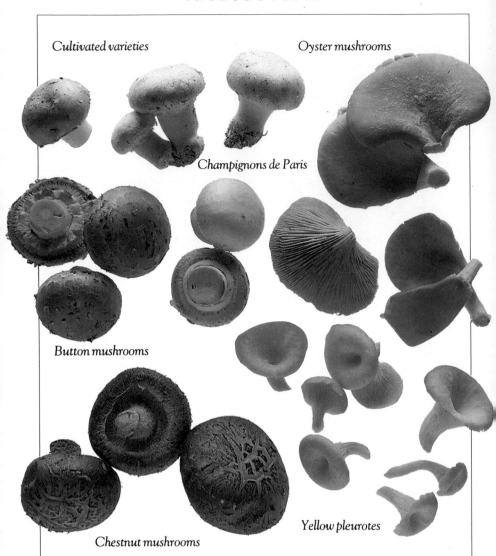

Cultivated varieties

Oyster mushrooms

Champignons de Paris

Button mushrooms

Chestnut mushrooms

Yellow pleurotes

When and Where They Grow

Mushrooms are magical. They have an uncanny habit of springing up, maturing and vanishing within the space of a few days or a couple of weeks. It can be bewildering. The cep has a growing cycle of about 2 weeks, whereas others appear and disappear within 24 hours. Some favour the same spot year after year, others do not. Their unpredictable nature adds to the excitement of the hunt, and to satisfaction in gathering them.

Most people believe that autumn is the only time to find mushrooms, but there are two excellent edible species – Morels (see page 44) and St George's Mushroom (see page 31) – which only appear in the spring, as well as Velvet Shank (see page 22), which can survive heavy frosts and be found in the middle of winter.

Mushroom enthusiasts are rather like farmers, always moaning about

the weather: "It's not a very good season – It's too dry – too warm – too cold" – or "there was a hard frost last night that will stop them growing". But despite such grumbles, you can usually find some fungi. They favour a combination of warmth and damp; a long, dry summer followed by a wet mild autumn encourages all kinds of mushrooms to burst out of the soil in profusion, whereas after a cold summer and a dry autumn they tend to be thin on the ground.

When mycologists (mushroom experts) refer to wood mushrooms, it does not mean you have to penetrate into the depths of some dark gloomy forest to find them; they need a certain amount of light and warmth and tend to favour the perimeters of the woods, and clearings.

Some species – such as *Suillus grevillus* (see page 40) will only grow in association with a particular tree; other fungi have a variety of hosts.

Field mushrooms grow on established pastures which have been grazed by horses, cows or sheep, because they rely on well manured soil for their nutrients.

Collecting

People think that you have to get up at the crack of dawn to collect mushrooms, but in fact any time of day will do. The only advantage of going mushrooming first thing in the morning is that you can gather field mushrooms, russulas or ceps before insects have had their share.

Buy a reliable field guide with good illustrations so that you can become familiar with all types of fungi. It is worth learning to recognize all the inedible ones to avoid possible confusion.

Take a flat-bottomed basket, with a selection of small containers to keep the different species apart. Do not put the fungi in your pockets or a carrier bag, as they can be easily damaged and are liable to sweat and start rotting.

If you are a beginner, it is a good idea to go out collecting with an experienced companion, or join an organized foray run by the local natural history group. You will learn a lot and have the peace of mind that comes from knowing your collection has been verified by an expert.

It is preferable to gather mushrooms in dry weather. Do not pick very young specimens which have not developed their distinguishing characteristics, nor old maggoty ones. Never cut through the stalk. You must take care to ensure that you get the whole stem from beneath the ground for full identification: to see whether the base of the mushroom tapers, or if it is bulbous, or perhaps encased by a bag-like sheath, known as a 'volva'.

The best way to pick a fungus is to twist it gently until it breaks free. Sometimes you will need a knife to loosen the soil around it, but take care not to damage the mycelium – the fine thread-like root system.

Note the cap shape, size, colour and texture. Check to see if the underneath has gills similar to the Field Mushroom (see page 12), a spongy mass of tubes and pores characteristic of *boletus* and related families (see pages 36-41), or spines like the Hedgehog Fungus (see page 43). If the mushroom has gills note the colour and whether they are decurrent – descending down the stem. Look at the margin – the edge of the cap: is it smooth, flared, wavy or in-rolled? Does the cap have a raised bump in the centre, known as a boss?

Study the stem carefully, too. Does it have a ring around it, and is the ring floppy, soft or even double?

Check whether the fungus bruises when touched, and break the flesh to see if it exudes a milky juice like the Saffron Milk Cap (see page 26).

Smell is the hardest thing to ascertain, apart from the Horse Mushroom (see page 13) which smells of aniseed, and *Russula xerampelina* (see page 33), which has a distinct crabby smell. The rest have a faint aroma which is easily masked.

When you gather tree species, generally known as bracket fungi, you must prize them off the wood gently with a knife then, as with other mushrooms, check all the salient features.

When you get home, double-check your identification before you slice them up and add them to the frying-pan. Be 100 per cent certain that you know what exactly you have collected, because mushroom poisoning is extremely painful.

Preparation

The best way to clean mushrooms is to wipe them with a damp cloth to remove any surplus dirt. Separate the stem from the cap to see if they are hiding a host of invading insects; the stalks tend to become maggot-ridden first. Do not peel mushrooms – the skin contains a lot of the nutritional goodness and flavour.

It is considered a crime to wash mushrooms, but with some species – such as Morels (see page 44) and Cauliflower Fungus (see page 50) – it is necessary because soil, pine needles and leaves get lodged in the holes, and a host of small insects can lurk in the folds and crevices.

If you are adding raw mushrooms to a salad or wish to prepare them in advance of cooking and do not want them to discolour, coat them with lemon juice.

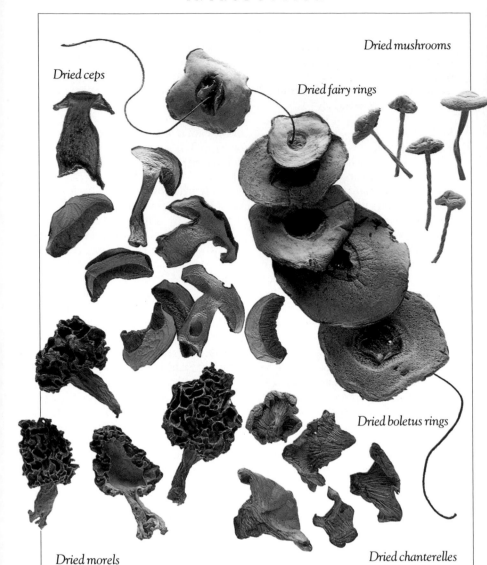

Dried ceps

Dried mushrooms

Dried fairy rings

Dried boletus rings

Dried morels

Dried chanterelles

Storing

Handle mushrooms as little as possible to avoid bruising them. Store in
a paper bag or punnet in the salad
compartment of the refrigerator. Do
not store them for more than a couple
of days however, because they do not
keep well.

Preserving

In a good season, when there is a glut
of mushrooms, you are bound to pick
more than you can eat. The best way
of preserving the flavour for a long
period is to dry them.

Use only very fresh mushrooms,
remove any blemishes and clean
thoroughly to remove all the dirt.
Cut large species, like *boletus*,
into thin slices, but leave small ones,
such as fairy ring mushrooms, whole.

If you live in a warm country you
will be able to sun-dry fungi. If you
live in a cool damp climate, you will

have to fix a wire rack above a
radiator or stove to place your mushrooms on. Allow a couple of days for
them to dry, shrink and become
brittle, then pack them in an airtight
jar.

You can dry mushrooms in a cool
oven with the door slightly ajar, but if
the temperature exceeds 60C (140F)
they will cook, blacken and lose their
flavour.

Alternatively, you can thread
mushrooms, particularly morels, on
fine string and hang them in an airing
cupboard or other warm place to dry.

To reconstitute dried mushrooms,
soak in warm water for 20-30 minutes.

If you have dried some of the
coarser mushrooms, it is better to
grind them to a powder and use this as
a flavouring; the concentrated
flavour is wonderful in soups and
vegetable dishes.

You can also preserve mushrooms by pickling in vinegar, or make ketchup.

To pickle, put the caps and stalks in a pan of salted water and bring to the boil. Remove from the heat and leave to stand for 5 minutes. Drain well and leave until cold and dry, then put into clean jars.

Simmer wine vinegar with whole peppercorns, bay leaves, fresh herbs, 1 onion and 2 bruised cloves garlic for 15 minutes. Leave to cool, then pour over the mushrooms to cover. Seal jars. Keep pickle for 2 to 3 weeks before using.

For a milder relish, make ketchup. Dice large mature caps and put in a pan. Scatter salt liberally over them and stir occasionally. Leave to stand for 2 days; add wine vinegar, finely chopped onions and garlic, peppercorns, ginger, nutmeg, cloves, cinnamon and allspice and simmer for about 2 hours. Strain, pour into hot sterilized jars and seal. This ketchup is ideal to serve with a cooked breakfast or it can be used to flavour other dishes. Once opened it must be used quickly.

Freezing
You can freeze mushrooms, but it is of limited value to do so because it diminishes their flavour, and they only keep for a month in the freezer.

Only use fresh, firm specimens: clean and open-freeze until solid; pack in plastic bags or containers to store.

The best way of freezing mushrooms, however, is to make a *duxelles*. Sauté a finely chopped onion and a crushed garlic clove in butter until softened. Finely slice the mushrooms, add to the pan and cook for 10 minutes or until dry. Season with salt, pepper, nutmeg and a handful of finely chopped parsley. Cool, transfer to a freezer-proof container, seal and freeze. Use from frozen as part of a filling for a chicken pie, as a flavouring for soups, stews and casseroles, or as a base for sauces.

Cooking
Mushrooms are virtually calorie-free. They are also rich in vegetable proteins and vitamin B. They are delicious raw – even better if they have been marinated in olive oil and herbs – and are lovely simply grilled or stewed in milk.

Mushrooms are very versatile and can be prepared with meat, game or fish, added to soups and sauces, or used on their own, stuffed, baked or, as the Japanese do, made into tempura fritters. All mushrooms, especially truffles, have an affinity with eggs, and ceps, chanterelles, and blewits are excellent cooked with potatoes. All species benefit from a squeeze of lemon juice while being sautéed – it helps to bring out their flavour.

Shaggy ink caps, chanterelles, parasol mushrooms and hedgehog fungi contain an enormous amount of water; when frying in butter, take care their juices do not spit. If there is an excessive amount of liquid, drain it off and reserve it for a stock.

If you are substituting wild species for their cultivated relatives, you will have to allow more mushrooms because of their higher moisture content and greater shrinkage. Their extra flavour compensates for their lack of size; this is particularly true of dried fungi. It can look very mean when you only soak 2 or 3 shrivelled slices, but their richness is sufficient to permeate a whole dish.

Using This Book
Nearly all the mushrooms described on the following pages grow wild in Britain. Many have distinctive features which make them easy to identify. To avoid repetition, where applicable I have noted the common characteristics shared by a particular family of mushrooms in the opening paragraph.

There are, in fact, very few poisonous fungi, and they are only mentioned if there is any possible likelihood of confusing them with an edible species. You should certainly avoid collecting Amanitas (page 42) unless you are an expert, because there are three lethal members belonging to this group. The photographs show clearly the many varieties which are safely edible. I strongly recommend you use this guide to edible mushrooms in conjunction with a well-illustrated field guide which will enable you to recognize inedible ones too.

½ life size

Agaricus bisporus

Field mushroom
(Agaricus campestris)

Field Mushroom

The Field Mushroom (*Agaricus campestris*) is the best known wild mushroom. Gone are the good old days when meadows were carpeted with white field mushrooms. They are still common in pastures, but tend to favour dense clumps of grass and only become visible when you are almost on top of them. You can find them from mid-summer through to autumn. They used to be sold in greengrocers and markets.

The field mushroom has a silky white turning cream coloured cap, 3-10 cm (1½-4 in) across. The pale pink gills turn reddish then brown when the button eventually opens. The stem tapers towards the base and has a delicate ring. It has a pleasant mushroom taste and smell.

Collecting and Storing
To collect field mushrooms you need to train your eyes to scan the ground a metre or so in front of you, because they are easy to miss or tread on nestling in the grass. Check there are no warts on the cap. If they have

pure white gills or stain yellow in the base of the stem, throw them away.

These mushrooms should be eaten fresh, but you can make ketchup with older black ones (see page 11).

Preparation and Cooking
Do not peel these mushrooms or their flavour will be slightly diminished; just wipe with a damp cloth and cut off the dirty base.

The best way to eat field mushrooms is to fry them in bacon fat as soon as you return home. For a decent meal you will need a panful; because of their high moisture content field mushrooms shrink to a third of their original volume.

Eat them on their own, or sauté with a little garlic; add breadcrumbs and spices and use the mixture to fill filo pastry parcels; or thicken their juices with egg yolks and cream to make a sauce. Field mushrooms are delicious served with shellfish, especially scallops.

The young buttons can be eaten raw, tossed into a green salad.

Agaricus bisporus

Parent of most cultivated varieties grown in Britain (see page 58), this mushroom can also be found growing on waste ground and compost heaps during the autumn. It is similar to the

field mushroom, but has a dirty buff coloured rather than white cap, 5-10 cm (2-4 in) across. It is good to eat and should be cooked in the same way as the field mushroom.

Horse Mushroom

A giant, meaty fungus recognizable by its distinct aniseed smell, the Horse Mushroom (*Agaricus arvensis*) is a large version of the field mushroom. It has a creamy-white cap and stem, which discolour and bruise yellow, unlike the field mushroom.

Great care must be taken not to confuse this mushroom with the toxic Yellow Stainer (*Agaricus xanthodermus*) which would make you violently ill if eaten. To differentiate between the two, ensure that you dig up the whole stem from under the ground, then cut through the base; if it turns bright yellow, you have the poisonous mushroom. If you have any doubts about your identification, don't eat it.

The horse mushroom can grow in vast quantities, often in rings, in old meadows or spinneys. It may reappear year after year in the same locality, from mid-summer through until mid-autumn. The young dome-shaped cap can expand up to 25 cm (10 in) across. The gills are white at first, turning a pinkish-grey, then chocolate-brown. The stem has a large floppy double ring. It has a strong mushroomy taste.

Collecting and Storing
Take extra care picking this species. Check the base to see if it turns yellow and sniff the cap for an aniseed scent. If you are confident you have found the horse mushroom, take it home and add it to the cooking pot. To get the maximum flavour, eat these mushrooms the day they are picked.

Preparation and Cooking
There is no need to peel horse mushrooms – just wipe away the dirt with a damp cloth. You can use the stems but they tend to be maggot-ridden, and become fibrous with age.

One large flat cap makes a hearty meal, especially cooked for breakfast. They are wonderful simply coated in a herb butter and grilled. Alternatively, because of their huge size, they are ideal to use as nests for stuffed quails – an unusual dish to serve at a dinner party.

If horse mushrooms are still dome-shaped, stuff them with a savoury filling and bake.

They can be used in most recipes but they are particularly good for croustades (see page 75).

Horse mushroom (Agaricus arvensis)

½ life size

Wood Mushroom

This woodland species has similar identifying characteristics to its big brother, the horse mushroom: it discolours and bruises yellow and has a distinct smell of aniseed. The Wood Mushroom (*Agaricus silvicola*) grows in coniferous and deciduous woods but favours beech and hornbeam. It is found from mid-summer through until the end of autumn.

This mushroom has a dry creamy white cap, 5-10 cm (2-4 in) across. The pinkish-grey gills darken with age to a chocolate-brown. It has a silky white stem with a button base and floppy ring attached.

Great care must be taken not to confuse it with the lethal Amanitas (see page 42) and the toxic Yellow Stainer (*Agaricus xanthodermus*).

Collecting and Storing

When gathering this mushroom, cut a couple of the young buttons in half to see if the flesh is yellow at the base and check to see if any of them have white gills; if either of these features are visible you will have picked the poisonous ones. If possible, get your identification verified by an expert before cooking.

Wood mushrooms should be eaten fresh as their flavour deteriorates with keeping.

Preparation and Cooking

Prepare and cook this tasty woodland species in the same way as field or horse mushrooms (see pages 12-13). The young caps are lovely coated in butter and deep-fried.

Agaricus Haemorrhoidarius

This mushroom is very similar in appearance to *Agaricus silvaticus* and *Agaricus langei* (see page 15), but is found in deciduous woods. The cap is covered in downy reddish-brown scales and the cut flesh turns red. It has a slightly bulbous stem with a broad ring attached. It grows under broad-leaved trees, especially beech and oak, during late summer and early autumn.

Collecting and Storing

Pick fresh young specimens. Like all *agarics* they should be eaten fresh; if you wish to preserve them freeze as a *duxelle* (see page 11).

Preparation and Cooking

Cut off most of the stalk and clean with a damp cloth. Fry with shallots, garlic and herbs, and serve on toast for a savoury snack.

Agaricus Silvaticus

The mature caps of this species look very similar to the field mushroom, although it prefers the shade. You can find *Agaricus silvaticus* growing in coniferous woods throughout the autumn.

The white cap is covered in tiny reddish-brown speckles and measures 5-10 cm (2-4 in) across. The gills are a pinkish-grey, becoming blackish with age. It has a rather scaley, bulbous stem which becomes hollow, and a floppy ring. The young buttons redden when they are cut but the older specimens, with brown flesh, do not discolour. Do not let this reddening put you off, because it is an excellent edible variety. It has a pleasant aroma, too.

Collecting and Storing

Only collect fresh young buttons because the larger ones tend to be infested with insects. They should be eaten fresh, but if you happen to find a glut of them, make them into *duxelle* and freeze (see page 11).

Preparation and Cooking

Use small buttons whole, but discard the tough, fibrous stalk from older specimens. Remove any dirt with a damp cloth.

These mushrooms are suitable to use in any mushroom dish. They can be made into soup, a sauce to serve with fish, added to pies and casseroles or, if you have only found a few, sliced and added to kedgeree.

Agaricus silvaticus

Agaricus haemorrhoidarius

*Wood mushroom
(Agaricus silvicola)*

¹/₂ *life size*

Agaricus Langei

This fungus is very similar to *Agaricus silvaticus* (opposite), but it grows in mixed woodland, in groups under spruce, sometimes oak. The cap is covered with dark brown scales, and the cut flesh immediately turns blood-red. It has a spindle-shaped stem with a large ring, and a pleasant mushroomy taste and smell. It is good to eat and well worth collecting; you should be able to find it from late summer through until the end of autumn. Treat the same as *Agaricus silvaticus*.

Honey Fungus

This fungus is very destructive in parks and gardens. It is responsible for killing all kinds of trees by causing white rot and eventual death. Honey Fungus (*Armillaria mellea*) is extremely common and can be found on living and dying trees, old stumps, buried branches or dead roots. It grows in large tufts from mid-summer through until late autumn.

This variable mushroom can have a honey coloured cap covered with dark scales, or it can be a rusty-red or dark brown, but whatever the hue it is usually darker in the centre. The size of the cap varies from 3-15 cm (1¼-6 in) across. The gills are creamy-yellow. The stem is white to yellow, sometimes spotted with rusty flecks, and it has a large soft ring. The base can be buttons and the stems often fuse together in clumps.

Honey fungus is also known as bootlace fungus because it is spread by means of long black cords called rhizomorphs which look like boot laces – you will always find them under the bark of infested trees.

A similar species, *Armillaria tabescens*, which also grows in clusters on old stumps, can be distinguished by its lack of a ring on the stem. It is edible, but must be cooked.

Collecting and Storing
Pick very young clusters. You can find this fungus in large quantities, but it does not keep well and is not worth drying.

Preparation and Cooking
Only eat the caps. Honey fungus should *never* be eaten raw and you must reject large old specimens because they can be very toxic and cause serious stomach upsets.

Many people enjoy eating this mushroom, but it does become rather soggy and slippery because it absorbs all the cooking fat or oil. It is not one of the best edible species but for some there is a certain vindictive pleasure to be gained from eating a fungus which destroys many of our beautiful trees!

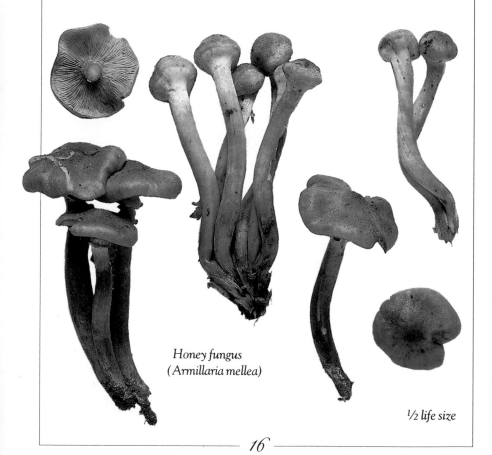

Honey fungus
(*Armillaria mellea*)

½ life size

Fairy ring mushroom (Marasius oreades)

Fairy Ring Mushroom

One of the most common grassland species, the Fairy Ring Mushroom (*Marasius oreades*) is found growing in large numbers in pastures and on lawns. As the name suggests, it often forms a ring. In fact, this fungus is much disliked by gardeners because it produces 'fairy rings' – bare circles bordered by dark grass appear where the mushrooms grew.

It is a well known reliable mushroom but great care should be taken to learn its characteristics to avoid mis-identification and confusion with a white one, *Clitocybe rivulosa*, which is poisonous.

Fairy ring mushrooms grow on slender, straw-coloured stems which are tough and leathery. The cap is a wide bell shape which expands as it matures and can be 2-5 cm (¾-2 in) across, but it always retains a small central boss. It can vary in colour from rusty-brown to tan when moist, drying a pale buff with a fawn centre. It smells slightly of hay.

Fairy rings can appear in late spring and continue growing until the end of autumn.

Collecting and Storing
Only gather fresh young mushrooms and pick the whole plant to ensure that you have the correct species. Fairy rings are ideal for drying, and seem to retain their flavour longer than other mushrooms. They are perfect to store for the winter, when they can be used to flavour soups, sauces and casseroles.

Preparation and Cooking
Discard the tough fibrous stem and wash the cap as little as possible. A basic method of cooking these delicious mushrooms is to fry them gently in butter with salt, pepper and a squeeze of lemon juice, then leave them to simmer for 15 minutes. They can be eaten on their own or added to an omelette.

Fairy ring mushrooms can be made into a cream of mushroom soup, thickened with egg yolks. They also add an interesting flavour to rice or minced steak fillings for peppers or large tomatoes, and taste delicious mixed into a rich butter and almond sauce to serve with baked fish.

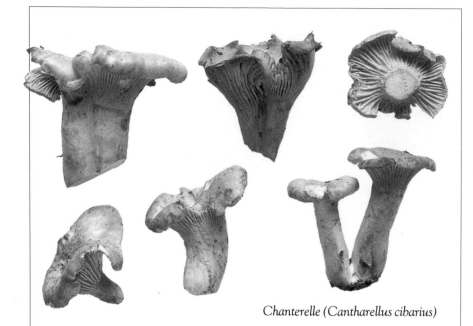

Chanterelle (Cantharellus cibarius)

Chanterelle

The Chanterelle (*Cantharellus cibarius*) is highly prized in Europe, especially in France, where it is commonly sold in markets and food stores and served in restaurants. Chanterelles rarely appear in British shops, although they grow quite freely throughout the British Isles.

These beautiful bright egg-yolk yellow mushrooms grow in all kinds of woods, preferring beech and oak. You can find them in clusters from mid-summer through until the beginning of winter. The bright funnel-shaped chanterelle turns a paler yellow as it dries.

The cap, which is depressed in the centre, has a curly edge and measures from 3-10 cm (1¼-4 in) across. Instead of gills the chanterelle has forked ridges – like veins – running halfway down the stem, which tapers towards the base. The chanterelle or *girolle*, as it is also called in France, smells of apricots and has a slightly fragrant taste.

Care must be taken not to confuse this fleshy mushroom with the False Chanterelle (*Hygophoropsis aurantiaca*) which is fragile in comparison, has ordinary gills, no smell, and is rather unpalatable.

Collecting and Storing

The bright yellow is easy to spot in mossy patches beneath leafy trees. Chanterelles grow in large groups so it is easy to gather a dozen or more; if you live in Scotland you will be able to pick basket-loads of them. Discard the muddy base so the mushrooms do not get covered in grit in the basket.

If you do not have time to go mushroom foraging, a few delicatessens import chanterelles from France, but they range widely in price depending on availability.

Chanterelles will stay fresh for up to a week if they are kept in the refrigerator. They can be dried but do not retain their flavour as well as some mushrooms.

Preparation and Cooking

Wipe the caps with a damp cloth and brush the dirt out of the ridges. These mushrooms are seldom attacked by insects, so it is only necessary to slice the larger ones lengthwise into strips. They give off a lot of liquid while cooking and reduce to about a third of their original volume.

Chanterelles have an affinity with eggs and potatoes, and are wonderful in sauces.

A simple method of preparation is to fry them slowly in butter or olive oil, with garlic and salt; just before serving, add chopped parsley, or some double (thick) cream to make a sauce of the juices, and use to fill an omelette or serve with salmon steaks. Chanterelles are also good cooked with bacon and potatoes.

Yellow Leg

The Yellow Leg (*Cantharellus infundibuliformis*) is fairly common in all types of woodland. Clusters of the dark brown caps are rather difficult to see, but if you find one it is worth ferreting around in the leaf litter as they often grow in large groups. They first appear in mid-summer and in a good year will continue growing until the beginning of winter.

The cap is slightly convex when young, becoming funnel-shaped with a wavy margin as it develops, and measures 2-5 cm (1½-2 in) across. The flesh is thin, and the fungus has narrow branching veins – yellowish at first, then grey – in place of gills. The veins descend down the compressed, dirty yellow stem. These mushrooms smell faintly aromatic but taste bitter and are unsavoury to eat raw.

Collecting and Storing
If you are lucky you should be able to gather quite a number of these mushrooms, but if you can only find a few, mix them with other collections. Before you put them in your basket, cut off the earthy base to keep them clean.

They will keep fresh in a refrigerator for up to a week. They are easy to dry and store for later use to flavour stews.

Preparation and Cooking
Wipe the caps with a damp cloth and brush away any grit embedded in the veins, or wash if necessary. Yellow legs are quite small so they can be used whole, although the stalks of older specimens will be leathery and rather chewy, and should therefore be removed.

Yellow legs need long slow cooking. Use them as you would chanterelles (see opposite); make into a sauce or add to egg dishes. They look attractive in a clear soup, and are tasty stir-fried with broccoli.

Yellow leg (Cantharellus infundibuliformis)

Horn of Plenty

Horn of Plenty (*Craterellus cornucopioides*), or Black Trumpet as it is sometimes called, is considered a great delicacy and is described in France as *la viande des pauvres*.

This fragile trumpet-shaped mushroom has a waxy, charcoal-grey outer surface, while the inside is a velvety blackish-brown. Perhaps because of its sombre colour, the French named this species *trompette de la mort*. Another characteristic feature is its lack of gills. The cap has a flared wavy margin and measures 2-7.5 cm (¾-3 in) across.

It can be found growing in large groups in damp deciduous woods, especially under oak or beech, during late summer and early autumn.

Collecting and Storing

It is very difficult to spot horn of plenty because of its ashen colour, but once you have found one it is worth searching through the leaf litter to find a good collection. It will stay fresh in the refrigerator for 4 to 5 days, but can be dried very easily and retains its flavour for later use in soups, stews or as a supplement to other mushroom dishes; it can also be powdered and used as a seasoning in soufflés or terrines.

If you are unable to find this mushroom growing, it is sold in some specialist shops throughout the autumn. It is also available dried.

Preparation and Cooking

Cut down one side so that you can open up the funnel and remove any dirt which has been trapped in the hollow stem with a brush or damp cloth.

Horn of plenty are delicious simply sautéed in butter for 15 minutes, with a squeeze of lemon juice; add a little cream and serve on toast for breakfast. They are also wonderful stir-fried with strips of green pepper and goujons of fish: halibut, cod or salmon. Alternatively, combine with a mixture of vegetables and bean sprouts; season with soy sauce.

Cantharellus Cinereus

These funnel-shaped mushrooms are rare in Britain. They bear a slight resemblance to horn of plenty, but are smaller, a brownish-grey rather than black, and have a compressed stem. They grow in clusters under broad-leaved trees, and are difficult to find among the leaf mould.

This is a good reliable species, and if you are fortunate enough to find some, cook them in a similar way to horn of plenty.

Cantharellus cinereus

Horn of plenty (Craterellus cornucopioides)

The Miller

The Miller (*Clitopilus prunulus*) is a very common mushroom which can be found growing in woodland glades and on heaths from mid-summer until the end of autumn. It has a strong mealy smell and taste which is reduced by cooking.

The miller has an irregular shaped cap, convex to depressed, 3-10 cm (1¼-4 in) across, which is often wavy at the edge. It has a white or pale cream matt 'suede' surface which turns greyish as it matures. The white gills descend down the stem and become pink with age.

Although this is a good reliable edible mushroom, great care must be taken not to confuse the miller with three poisonous species which closely resemble it: *Clitocybe dealbata*, *Clitocybe rivulosa* and the rarer *Entoloma sinuatum*.

Collecting and Storing
When you collect the miller, pick the whole mushroom and use a field guide to help identification. The miller smells and looks like the poisonous species named above. Ask an expert to check your identification and if there is any doubt leave it behind. It will stay fresh for a couple of days in the refrigerator.

Preparation and Cooking
Only use fresh, young specimens. Cut away the earthy base and wipe the cap with a damp cloth to remove any dirt.

Slice the mushrooms and fry in butter with a finely chopped onion and a handful of fresh herbs, such as marjoram, chives and thyme. When most of the juices have evaporated, add 2 tablespoons yogurt. Serve as a starter or on toast as a light snack. A slight variation to this dish is to add some garlic and use thick sour cream instead of yogurt.

Alternatively, cook the mushrooms in olive oil, with onions, garlic and tomatoes; season with black pepper and fresh basil; serve with spaghetti.

Some people find the strong mealy taste of this mushroom rather overpowering; if so, mix them with cultivated mushrooms.

Velvet Shank

As the English name implies, this species has a dark velvety stem. Velvet Shank (*Flammulina velutipes*) is one of the few mushrooms which can survive frost; it can be frozen solid and then revived on thawing. It grows during the winter months and, because of its late appearance, there is little chance of confusing it with other fungi.

It is a fairly common mushroom which grows in tufts on decaying stumps and dead branches, especially elm. If you have a wood fire you are just as likely to find it in your log pile as anywhere else. The sticky shiny cap is orange and honey-yellow, darkening towards the centre, and measures 2-10 cm (1¼-4 in) across. The gills are pale yellow. The stem is tan at the top and blackish-brown at the base, and covered in dense velvety hairs. It is rather fragile.

Velvet shanks smell and taste pleasant. They are valued because they occur when there are few other species available, although the Japanese regard them as a delicacy and cultivate them.

Collecting and Storing
Prize the clusters off the dead wood with a knife. The only way to store these mushrooms is to dry them and keep in an airtight jar until required.

Preparation and Cooking
Only use the tiny caps, after washing off the sticky coating. They can be sautéed in butter or added to casseroles, but they have a rather rubbery texture.

It is preferable to use the dried caps, powdered and added as a flavouring to soups and sauces just before serving.

The miller (Clitopilus prunulus)

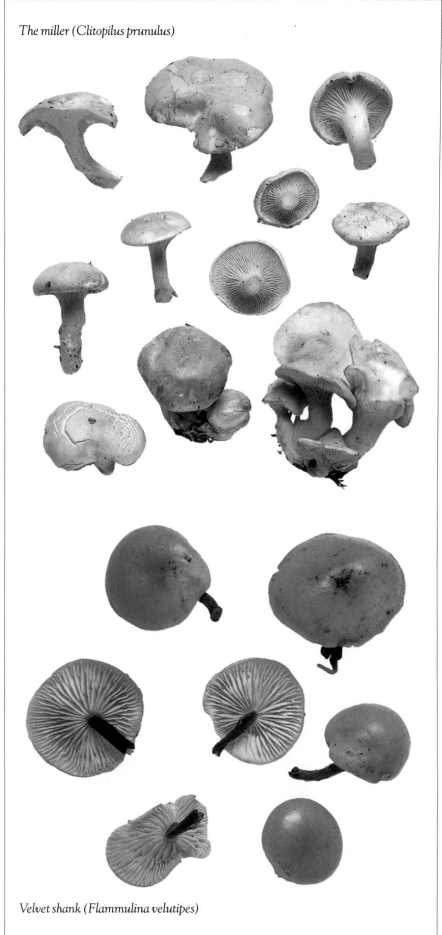

Velvet shank (Flammulina velutipes)

Shaggy Ink Cap

Common in fields, along grass tracks, on compost heaps, and recently disturbed ground, the Shaggy Ink Cap (*Coprinus comutus*) can be found in vast quantities. However it is more typically seen growing in small tufts on lawns or roadside verges during summer and autumn.

This mushroom is also called Inky Top and Lawyer's Wig, because its cylindrical white cap, which is 5-15 cm (2-6 in) tall, is covered with feathery curls like a judge's wig. As the cap matures, it becomes limp, the white gills turn pink, then black as they begin to dissolve, leaving a dripping button on top of a long, smooth white stem, which has a tiny white ring when young. Shaggy ink caps have a mild, pleasant taste.

Collecting and Storing
Shaggy ink caps are extremely fragile and you should only gather young ones, with closed caps and white gills, for eating. They need to be cooked as quickly as possible after picking because they start to disintegrate within a couple of hours.

The only way to preserve these mushrooms is to turn them into ketchup (see page 11).

Preparation and Cooking
To prepare shaggy ink caps, discard the hollow stem. Wipe the caps carefully to remove any dirt, but do not wash them as they are liable to collapse.

Add the white caps to a chicken or vegetable stock to make a thin delicate soup. Season with salt and pepper, enrich with cream, and sprinkle with finely chopped parsley just before serving.

Shaggy ink caps are delicious baked in the oven with a knob of butter, a finely chopped shallot, a hint of garlic and seasoning, and eaten while piping hot with homemade bread to mop up the juices.

Alternatively, cut the caps lengthwise into strips and lightly cook in butter. Serve on toast, or place the slivers and their juices on top of eggs in individual buttered ramekins, put in a *bain-marie* and bake in a moderate oven.

Shaggy ink caps are excellent with fish, especially turbot, sole and whiting. They can be added to the fish before it is battered and fried; or made into a light sauce, by adding a small carton of single (light) cream, to serve with grilled fish.

Common Ink Cap

The Common Ink Cap (*Coprinus atramentarius*) is distinguished from its cousin by its shorter, smooth, dirty grey coloured cap, 3-7 cm (1¼-2¾ in) tall. The gills are white, turning black as it rots.

It is this mushroom that gave the group its name, because at one time ink was made by boiling the blackened caps with water and cloves.

It is found growing in clusters near the base of trees in fields and parks from spring through to late autumn.

The young buttons with white gills are delicious, but they must not be eaten with alcohol because the combination will cause palpitations and vomiting.

Glistening Ink Cap

The Glistening Ink Cap (*Coprinus micaceus*) with its short tawny brown cap, 1-4 cm (½-1¾ in) high, is covered with a fine boundary dust when young. It is also considered edible but hardly worth collecting.

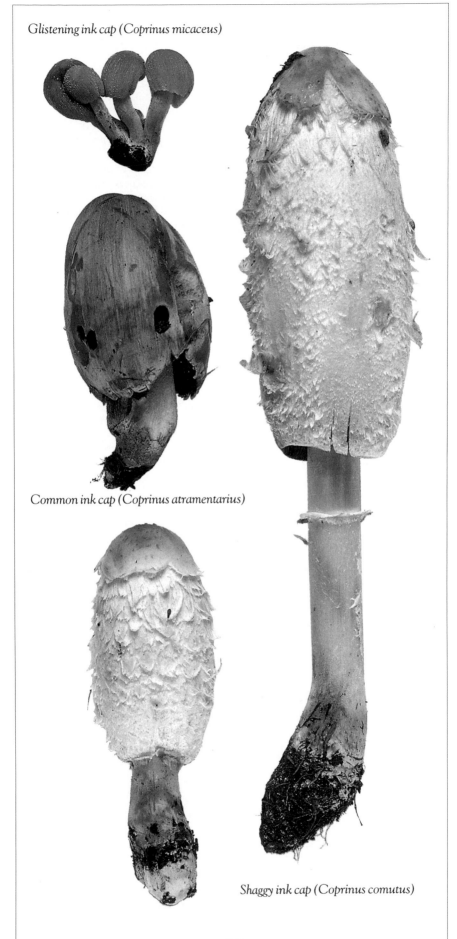

Glistening ink cap (*Coprinus micaceus*)

Common ink cap (*Coprinus atramentarius*)

Shaggy ink cap (*Coprinus comutus*)

Saffron Milk Cap

The Saffron Milk Cap (*Lactarius deliciosus*) is much sought after in Europe, especially in France, where it is collected in vast numbers and canned. In Britain it is largely ignored.

This is a thick, fleshy, bright orange species when young which becomes spotted green with age. The cap measures 3-10 cm (1¼-4 in) across, and is convex or slightly funnel-shaped. The vivid gills are decurrent – running down – into a stout salmon-coloured stem covered with dark orange blotches.

Like all members of *Lactarius*, the saffron milk cap exudes a milky liquid when the stem is cut or the gills are crushed; this one weeps a sweet orange milk which has a bitter after-taste.

This mushroom grows in pine forests in Scotland during late summer and early autumn. If you are fortunate enough to find a spot where it grows in England, you are likely to find it in large quantities.

Saffron milk cap is not quite as delicious as its botanical name would lead you to assume; it has a mild, slightly bitter flavour. It is, however, the only member of its family worth cooking. Some dispute this, claiming that its cousin, *Lactarius deterrimus*, is good to eat. It looks very similar to the saffron milk cap, but has a smooth, unmarked stem, and the milk turns purple after 10 minutes. It is rare, but you can sometimes find it growing under spruce or pine trees. It has a rather acid, soapy taste.

Collecting and Storing
Only pick young specimens, as the older ones tend to be infested with insects. Carefully wipe, or wash if necessary, to remove surface dirt.

This mushroom will keep for several days in the refrigerator.

Preparation and Cooking
A lovely way to cook these mushrooms is to slice them and fry in olive oil with a garlic clove until light brown, then add some white wine, a mixture of fresh herbs and lemon juice; cook until the liquid has reduced to a good thick sauce. Eat immediately with fresh crusty bread.

Alternatively, add the cooked mushrooms to a cream and Madeira sauce and serve with pork tenderloin. They can also be added to a blanquette of lamb.

Curry-Scented Milk-Cap

This mushroom is worth mentioning because, although it is rather unpalatable to eat fresh, dried and powdered it has a strong spicy, curry taste and aroma, and makes a good seasoning.

The Curry-Scented Milk-Cap (*Lactarius camphoratus*) is usually found in groups under pine trees, but sometimes you can find it in deciduous woods during late summer and autumn. It has a matt, chestnut-brown cap, 2.5-5 cm (1-2 in) across, which is slightly depressed, but often has a small hump in the centre. The gills are decurrent and closely spaced. The milk is quite watery and has a mild flavour.

Saffron milk cap (Lactarius deliciosus)

Parasol Mushroom

You can often pick your first Parasol (*Lepiota procera*) at the height of summer. They are a welcome find and usually herald the beginning of the mushroom season. Parasols can grow in the same spot year after year, and in a good season there will be several flushes which you can crop.

The parasol is one of the best edible species, with a delicious nutty flavour. It is found in woodland glades, on parkland, heaths, along grassy banks bordering estuaries and cliff tops, from mid-summer until the middle of autumn.

This tall, distinctive mushroom can easily be spotted because of its preference for open spaces. The young specimens look like drum sticks, but as they mature the cap expands like an umbrella and can grow as large as 40 cm (16 in) across. The pale buff cap is covered with feathery dark brown scales and has a central boss. The brittle gills are creamy white. The hollow, slender stem grows out of a bulbous base; it is covered with a snake-skin pattern and has a loose ring.

Collecting and Storing
Ideally you should only pick parasols when the cap is just beginning to open, but it is difficult to resist the large parasols because they look so wonderful. Do not gather any that have started to dry out because they will be too leathery to eat.

They are best eaten the day you collect them, but they will keep in the refrigerator for a couple of days. These mushrooms can be dried, but tend to lose some of their flavour.

Preparation and Cooking
Discard the fibrous stalks. Carefully wipe caps with a damp cloth; only wash if necessary.

The cup-shaped caps are ideal for stuffing – with a sage and onion mixture, for example – and baking. My favourite way of preparing parasols, especially if found during the summer, is to coat them with an anchovy and parsley butter and grill them over a charcoal barbecue.

The large caps can be quartered and made into fritters, or simply fried and served for breakfast with bacon and eggs.

Shaggy Parasol

The Shaggy Parasol (*Lepiota rhacodes*) is short and stocky in comparison to its elegant big brother. It tastes just as delicious, although some people tend to be rather squeamish about this species because when the flesh is cut it turns a reddish colour. This mushroom is strongly aromatic.

The shaggy parasol prefers to grow in shady areas, and can be found in woods, shrubberies and on garden compost heaps during summer and autumn. It is more common than the parasol mushroom.

The creamy buff cap is coated with curly brownish-red scales and varies between 5-15 cm (2-6 in) across. It has a thick, smooth stem which is whitish with pink-brown tinges, and it has a thick, moveable ring. The base is large and bulbous.

Collecting and Storing
Gather only firm young specimens and cut away the earthy base before putting them in your basket. This fleshy mushroom will stay fresh for up to a week in the refrigerator. It is also suitable for drying.

Preparation and Cooking
Discard the tough stem, which is inedible. Wipe or wash the cap to remove any surface dirt.

The shaggy parasol can be prepared in the same way as the parasol mushroom: stuffed, made into fritters, fried and eaten for breakfast, or served as a vegetable in a cream sauce. It is particularly good baked with Madeira. The large caps can be used to excellent effect as a base on which to serve quail's eggs, with bacon, endive and chives.

Parasol mushroom (*Lepiota procera*)

Shaggy parasol (*Lepiota rhacodes*)

¹/₃ *life size*

Oyster Mushroom

The Oyster Mushroom (*Pleurotus ostreatus*) grows virtually all year, on rotten stumps and fallen trunks of deciduous trees, especially beech and ash, except when it is very cold. It is a well known edible species, which is now grown commercially in Europe and is available in the shops (see below). It is more fun to collect your own, though.

The oyster mushroom grows in clusters of overlapping tiers, like tiles, on decaying wood. As its common name suggests, the cap is shell-shaped and measures 6-14 cm (2½-5½ in) across. It is extremely variable in colour, ranging from cream to fawn, to grey-brown, or deep slate grey-blue. The gills are white, discolouring yellow, and they run down into a short solid stem. It is best to gather oyster mushrooms in the late summer and autumn.

Collecting and Storing
This mushroom is well worth collecting. It has the added attraction of growing in large clumps so you can usually pick enough for a decent meal. Only prize really young clusters from branches or stumps, because they get very tough as they mature.

You can dry these mushrooms, but it is preferable to eat them fresh.

CULTIVATED OYSTER MUSHROOM
Oyster mushrooms have recently started to be cultivated. It is a secretive business, and if you visit a farmer he will not allow you into his growing sheds from fear that you might reveal some of his dark secrets.

Oyster mushrooms are not grown on elaborately prepared trays of manure, but on roundish cushions of compacted straw, sawdust and compost, which are encased by a plastic mesh. Farmers have tried to emulate their natural growing conditions by placing the discs on top of each other. When the mycelium, a white thread-like mass, spreads over the surface, the mesh is removed to allow the mushrooms to grow out from the sides and form their true fan-shape.

The cultivated varieties often have longer stems than their wild counterparts and mature specimens tend to become funnel-shaped.

Farmers are nurturing the fawn, slate grey-blue and a new yellow variety, which until now has only been grown in France. These are labelled Yellow Pleurotes, but they lose their wonderful colour when they are cooked.

Buying and Storing
Cultivated oyster mushrooms are widely available. In many ways it is preferable to buy pre-packed rather than loose mushrooms, because this fragile species is easily broken, whilst those in punnets remain whole. Most of the oyster mushrooms in British shops are imported from France and Holland, but some are home-produced.

Always choose young firm specimens. They will keep fresh for 3 to 4 days in the refrigerator. They may be dried or powdered.

Preparation and Cooking
Treat wild and cultivated specimens in exactly the same way. You can eat the whole mushroom – just wipe with a damp cloth to remove any dirt.

Oyster mushrooms can be eaten raw but some people find them rather indigestible. They can be added to most recipes and used in place of any of the cultivated mushrooms. They are good to fry, grill and bake.

Coated in a crispy batter, oyster mushrooms are lovely to dip into a thick sour cream and lemon balm sauce. As with most fungi, they are delicious cooked with Madeira and cream, served on their own garnished with parsley, in vol-au-vent or tartlet cases, or as a sauce with pork tenderloin. Alternatively, poach them whole in wine with Dover sole, saving a few to add to the sauce made from the juices.

$^1/_3$ life size

Oyster mushroom (Pleurotus ostreatus)

Cultivated oyster mushroom

Yellow pleurote

Russulas

There are some extremely colourful members of this family: bright red, purple, chrome yellow or green, in addition to the more familiar brown hues. This ought to make identification easier, but there are so many of them, and each species is so variable, that it is hard to distinguish one from the other.

Illustrated here are four popular edible *russulas*, but it is advisable to consult an expert to check your identification – it is better to be over-cautious and healthy rather than too confident and ill. However, none of the mushrooms in this group are seriously poisonous.

THE CHARCOAL BURNER
Probably the most common species, the Charcoal Burner (*Russula cyanoxantha*) can be found throughout Britain under broad-leaved trees, especially beech. It can appear from early summer until the middle of autumn.

The flat cap can grow up to 15 cm (6 in) across, and as it matures it tends to become depressed at the centre. It can be a single colour – steely blue, grey, purple or greenish – or a mixture. The stem is white and firm. This fleshy *russula* has a mushroomy smell and mild, nutty taste. It is sometimes on sale in European markets.

YELLOW SWAMP RUSSULA
A colourful mushroom, Yellow Swamp Russula (*Russula claroflava*) is relatively easy to identify. It is common in damp birch woods, but also favours alder and aspen, and is usually found growing in mossy areas during late summer and autumn.

The shiny bright yellow cap, 4-10 cm (1½-4 in) across, fades with age; it is rather sticky and you should be able to peel the skin halfway back. The gills are creamy-yellow and the stem is white, but when touched it bruises grey. Although is has a strong fruity smell, this mushroom has a mild taste. It adds colour to most recipes and is ideal to mix with other species.

½ life size

Charcoal burner (Russula cyanoxantha)

Yellow swamp russula (Russula claroflava)

Russula xerampelina

Green-cracked russula
(*Russula virescens*)

½ life size

GREEN-CRACKED RUSSULA

Connoisseurs consider the Green-cracked Russula (*Russula virescens*) to be the best member of the family to eat, but unfortunately it is rather difficult to find. It grows in grass under broad-leaved trees, especially around beech, during summer and autumn.

This *russula* has a dry dull, grey-green, blue-green or olive-green cap, 5-10 cm (2-4 in) across, and the skin tends to crack into small scales showing white below. It has a short, fleshy white stem which browns slightly with age. The mature cap has a mild nutty smell and flavour, but when young they taste more like fresh potatoes which makes them particularly suitable to add to potato recipes.

RUSSULA XERAMPELINA

Russula xerampelina tends to grow in mixed woods, particularly near oak and beech, and can be found from mid-summer until late autumn. It has a dry, slightly depressed cap of varying hues of pink, purple or brown with a blackish centre, measuring 5-12 cm (2-4½ in) across. The stem is white or rose tinted.

The characteristic feature of this *russula* is its distinctive smell of crab, which even persists after it has been cooked. This makes it especially suited to seafood dishes.

Collecting and Storing Russulas

Squirrels have a penchant for the colourful caps, while grubs like the fleshy stems, so collect young buttons before the woodland fauna have had their feast. *Russulas* are rather brittle and should be placed in a punnet to prevent them breaking.

These mushrooms are best eaten fresh, but can be preserved in vinegar (see page 10).

Preparing and Cooking Russulas

With fresh young specimens use the whole mushroom, but discard the stalks of older ones. Wash off any leaves which have stuck to the cap under running cold water.

Russulas retain their firm texture when cooked. You can grill or bake them, or stuff them with roast pecans, breadcrumbs, shallots and cheese, adding seasoning and a squeeze of lemon juice.

A mixture of *russulas*, gently fried in butter with onions, garlic and seasoning, and served on toast is delicious. Russulas are also lovely served with a cream sauce and eaten with pasta.

The green-cracked russula is the only one which can be eaten raw: toss in green salads, and use in marinades.

St George's mushroom (Tricholoma gambosum)

St George's Mushroom

A springtime mushroom, St. George's Mushroom (*Tricholoma gambosum*) is never found in the autumn. As the name implies, you would naturally assume that you would find this species in England on St. George's Day, 23rd April, but unless it has been exceptionally warm it does not usually appear until a couple of weeks later. It is common on chalky grassland, at wood edges and roadsides, and is often found growing in large fairy rings during late spring and early summer.

St. George's mushroom bears a slight resemblance to the cultivated mushroom. It has a thick fleshy cap, 5-15 cm (2-6 in) across, with an inrolled margin, which is white, discolouring cream or apricot. The gills and stem are white. This species has a distinctive mealy smell and taste which is brought out to the full in soups.

Collecting and Storing

Only pick fresh young buttons, because the strong mealy taste is rather overpowering in the large old specimens. They will keep fresh in the refrigerator for a day or two. This mushroom is not really worth drying because it does not retain its flavour.

Preparation and Cooking

St. George's mushrooms can be substituted for cultivated mushrooms and used in most recipes. Cut off the earthy base and wipe the cap with a damp cloth to remove any dirt.

To prepare, simply slice and fry them in butter with pepper, salt and a dash of lemon juice. Serve on toast for a light snack, or use this mixture as an omelette filling. To enrich this simple recipe, add crushed garlic, thick sour cream and fresh herbs; this makes a tasty savoury filling for vol-au-vents, to serve warm or cold with aperitifs.

To bring out the full flavour of St. George's mushrooms, use them to make a soup, thickened with cream and egg yolks.

Field Blewit

The Field Blewit (*Lepista saeva*), also called blue leg, is one of the best edible species – far superior to the wood blewit – but it is difficult to find. It is one of the few wild mushrooms to be eaten in Britain, especially in the Midlands, where it is sometimes sold at local markets.

You find field blewits in old grassy pastures, often growing in large rings. They are easy to miss because their dull grey-brown, wavy caps look like shrivelled leaves wedged between the grass. The caps measure 5-10 cm (2-4 in) across. The gills are flesh coloured and the stem creamy, with a distinct bluish-mauve tinge, hence the common name. They may have a swollen base.

Field blewits can tolerate a certain amount of cold weather and appear during autumn and early winter. They have a strong perfumed smell and taste.

Collecting and Storing

Pick these mushrooms on a dry day because the porous caps become slimy in wet weather. They will keep for a day or two in the refrigerator.

Preparation and Cooking

Use the whole mushroom, removing dirt with a damp cloth. This fragrant mushroom is superb combined with chicken in a white sauce and used as a pie filling. Alternatively, bake the large caps with a savoury mixture which includes the diced stalk.

Wood Blewit

A bluish-lilac mushroom which turns brown with age, the Wood Blewit (*Lepista nuda*) is common in mixed woodland and gardens during autumn and early winter. Unlike its cousin, it has purple gills which fade to a light brown. The cap measures 6-12 cm (2½-4½ in) across. Fresh wood blewits have a sweet perfumed smell and taste, but once they have been cooked the flavour is similar to that of new potatoes.

Collecting and Storing

This mushroom can be kept in the refrigerator for a day or two.

Preparation and Cooking

Wood blewits should not be eaten raw because they are slightly toxic, and some people are allergic to them. Parboil them before incorporating in a recipe.

Cook in the same ways as field blewits; add to potatoes *au gratin*.

Wood blewit (Lepista nuda)

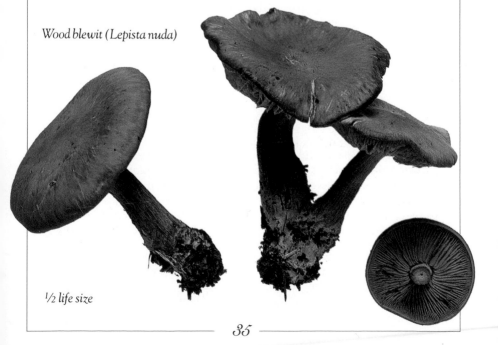

½ life size

½ life size

Cep (Boletus edulis)

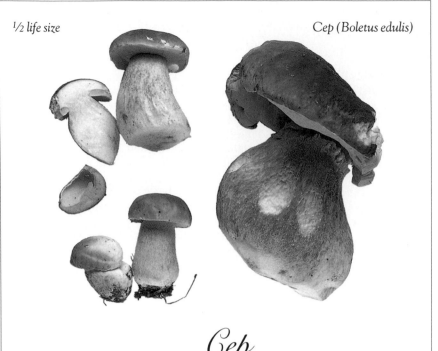

Cep

The cep is a member of the *Boletus* family, whose main characteristic is that they have tubes – a spongy layer covered with tiny pores – instead of gills.

King of the edible mushrooms, the Cep (*Boletus edulis*) is avidly searched for in Europe, especially in Italy where it is collected in vast quantities and dried for the winter. Sadly, it is neglected in Britain, although it is common in woodland glades, particularly near beech trees, during summer and autumn.

The French call this mushroom 'cep' because its fat stem looks like a trunk. In Britain it is known as the 'penny bun' because the sticky brown cap resembles one, but I have yet to fathom why the Italians refer to it as *porcini*, which translates as piglets! Whatever name you adopt, this mushroom has a delicious nutty flavour.

The cep has a brownish cap, 8-20 cm (3-8 in) across, which becomes greasy in damp weather. It has cream to olive-yellow pores and a thick bulging fawn stem which is partially covered with a fine network pattern.

Collecting and Storing

Pick fresh specimens with firm caps; these will stay fresh in the refrigerator for about a week.

Ceps are excellent for drying, as they retain their flavour and a small amount goes a long way.

If you are unable to find any growing wild, you can sometimes buy fresh ceps from specialist greengrocers during the autumn.

Dried *porcini* are available all year from delicatessens. Old ones blacken, so only buy cream and browny coloured ones which have been recently imported.

Preparation and Cooking

Small grubs are fond of these sought-after mushrooms so it is wise to cut them in half or remove the stalk to see if they are infested. Clean them with a damp cloth, and scoop away the pores if they have turned a yellowish green.

There are numerous ways of cooking ceps. The large caps can be filled with ham or bacon, shallots, herbs, breadcrumbs and grated Parmesan cheese, brushed with a little oil and baked. Or simply fry in olive oil and add crushed garlic and parsley just before serving. They can be made into a sauce to accompany pasta – Italians even fill ravioli with them.

The young caps are delicious eaten raw in a green or seafood salad.

If you have any left over, preserve them in a herb marinade for later use – they are excellent served as an hors d'oeuvre.

Bay Boletus

Another delicious member of the *boletus* family, the Bay Boletus (*Boletus badius*) is common throughout Britain during autumn. It grows in coniferous woods, but can occasionally be spotted under deciduous trees.

This mushroom has a bay to chocolate-brown felty cap, 4-14 cm (1½-5½ in) across, which becomes rather clammy when it gets wet. It is smaller than the cep and lacks the fine network on the stem.

An identifiable feature of this mushroom is that the lemon-yellow pores bruise a blue-grey when touched. The slender stem is white at the top with brown markings below. Bay boletus has a mild,

mushroomy taste and smell.

Collecting and Storing
Gather young specimens with firm caps. They will stay fresh for a week in the refrigerator and, like the cep, are ideal to dry.

Preparation and Cooking
This species is not eaten by woodland grubs so there is no need to remove the stalk prior to cleaning with a damp cloth.

Cook in a similar way to ceps (opposite) or if you have only managed to find a few, use to flavour sautéed potatoes. Alternatively, they are lovely cooked in cream and added to an omelette.

Red-cracked Boletus

The Red-cracked Boletus (*Boletus chrysenteron*) is found throughout Britain in deciduous woods, especially growing in grass under beech and oak, but it is not one of the best to eat.

The distinguishing feature of this *boletus* is that the velvety tan to olive-brown cap surface cracks to reveal yellow or coral flesh beneath. The cap measures 4-11 cm (1½-4½ in) across. The pale yellow

pores turn greenish with age; the stem is yellow at the top, with a rosy-red base. The cut flesh slowly turns bluish; it has a mild smell and taste.

Collecting and Storing
Although this mushroom is not really suitable for cooking because it turns mushy, it is worth collecting for drying, as it retains its flavour well. Pick firm young specimens.

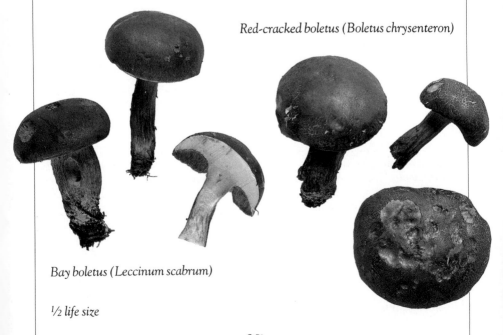

Red-cracked boletus (*Boletus chrysenteron*)

Bay boletus (*Leccinum scabrum*)

½ life size

Brown Birch Boletus

All members of the *Leccinum* genus have dry caps and woolly scaly stems; they are often called 'rough stalks'. All are edible.

The Brown Birch Boletus (*Leccinum scabrum*) is the most prolific of these tall-stemmed *boletus*, but unfortunately it is not particularly good to eat. It is common, growing in grass under birch trees, and can be found throughout the summer and autumn.

The velvety cap, 5-15 cm (2-6 in) across, is hazel to snuff-brown and becomes slimy when wet. The cream pores discolour grey. The firm white stem is covered in rough dark brown scales. The flesh does not change colour when it is cut. It has a mild smell and taste.

Collecting and Storing
Gather firm young specimens only, because the mature caps are spongy. The best way to store this mushroom is to dry and powder it.

Preparation and Cooking
The brown birch boletus is often maggoty, so only use the caps. If the pores feel squidgy, discard them and wipe the caps with a damp cloth. These mushrooms are only suitable for making soup.

Leccinum Quercinum

This mushroom is rare and only grows under oaks. If you happen to live in Southern England you might be lucky enough to find it from mid-summer until the middle of autumn.

Leccinum quercinum has a brick-red cap, 6-15 cm (2½-6 in) across, and has been nicked-named the 'brick cap'. The thick stem is coated by a fine network of orange scales. The pores are buff, becoming darker with age. If the stem is cut the flesh turns a pink-grey. This mushroom has a pleasant smell and taste and is good to eat.

Collecting and Storing
If you find one *Leccinum quercinum*, it is worth searching around neighbouring oaks because, although they appear only singly or in pairs, they can be scattered over a large area. This is a robust species, fairly bug free, so it is safe to collect mature ones. Like their cousins, these mushrooms are excellent dried.

Preparation and Cooking
Clean with a damp cloth and cut away the base of the stalk. Cook in similar ways as ceps (see page 36).

Orange Birch Boletus

Recognizable by the striking orange or yellowish-red cap, the Orange Birch Boletus (*Leccinum versipelle*) commonly grows in grass under birch. It can be found throughout the summer and autumn.

This is the tallest mushroom of the family and the cap can measure up to 20 cm (8 in) across. The pores are grey at first, then white and finally dirty yellow, bruising blue-grey. The stem is often club-shaped and is covered with woolly brown scales. The flesh blackens when it is cut up and cooked, but do not be put off by this because it is a good edible species.

A close relative, *Leccinum auran-tiacum*, has a downy, apricot to brown coloured cap, 8-16 cm (3-6½ in) across, with a tall stem covered with rusty-brown scales. The cut flesh turns pinky-grey and gradually blackens. Although this mushroom is good to eat, it is rare and only grows under poplars during summer and autumn.

Collecting and Storing
Pick mushrooms with firm caps. The orange birch boletus is ideal for drying and powdering, because it retains its flavour. In dried form, it is ideal to keep for use during the winter, to season soups, terrines or mushroom dishes.

Brown birch boletus (Leccinum scabrum)

Orange birch boletus (Leccinum versipelle)

Leccinum quercinum

¹/₂ life size

Preparation and Cooking

The fibrous stems are too tough to eat, so only use the caps. If the pores have become a dirty yellow and feel soggy, discard them; they are easy to detach and peel away from the cap. Clean the mushrooms with a damp cloth.

The large caps are ideal to fill with a savoury stuffing and bake. Make the small caps into a sauce to serve with pasta or, if they are firm and saucer-shaped, pour a few drops of olive oil into the centre, add some fresh herbs, crushed garlic and a dash of lemon juice, wrap in foil and cook over a barbecue. If you have only a few orange birch boletus mix them with other mushrooms, preferably ceps.

Suillus

All of this family can be found in coniferous woods. Most have shiny sticky caps, and all have pores and spongy flesh instead of gills.

Suillus are flavoursome but not good eaten fresh because they absorb all the fat or oil in which they have been cooked and become soggy and slimy. However, they are well worth gathering for drying to be used as a flavouring for soups, sauces, stews and fricassés.

SLIPPERY JACK
Slippery Jack *(Suillus luteus)* is the largest member of the group. It has a chestnut-brown cap, 5-12 cm (2-4½ in) across, which is coated with a shiny lilac-tinted glutin. It has lemon-yellow pores and the stem is a dirty yellow colour with a large floppy brownish-purple ring. This species prefers to grow on sandy soil and it can be found in abundance in Scots pine plantations during summer and autumn.

Although it is a good edible fungus to collect, it is prone to be eaten by bugs, especially during the warm weather, so it is advisable to pick it later in the season. Its taste and smell are not distinctive.

SUILLUS BOVINUS
Suillus bovinus is common in conifer woods, especially in damp areas, during summer and autumn. The sticky, pinkish-tawny cap, 3-10 cm (1¼-4 in) across, has a distinct white margin. It has large greenish-yellow pores and the stem is the same colour as the cap. It has a fruity smell and tastes pleasant.

SUILLUS VARIEGATUS
Suillus variegatus can be found in mixed coniferous forests during summer and autumn. The mustard coloured cap, 6-13 cm (2½-5 in) across, is felty and speckled with rust to dark brown scales. It is sticky only in wet weather. The pores are olive green tinged with blue. The firm stem is a similar colour to the cap. It has a strong smell but a mild taste.

LARCH BOLETUS
The Larch Boletus *(Suillus grevilles)*, also known as *Boletus elegans*, grows exclusively in grass under larch trees, and can be harvested in large quantities during summer and autumn. The tacky golden cap, 3-10 cm (1¼-4 in) across, darkens to a rusty orange as it matures, and it is shiny when dry. The pores are lemon yellow and bruise brownish when touched. The yellow stem is tinged with orange and it has a whitish ring. This mushroom has a mild smell and taste.

SUILLUS GRANULATUS
Suillus granulatus is common on sandy soil in coniferous woods throughout the summer and autumn. It has a glutinous reddish-brown cap, 3-9 cm (1¼-3½ in) across, which is shiny when dry and is easy to peel. The lemon pores exude tiny milky droplets. The upper section of the whitish to pale yellow stem is covered in granules, hence the name.

Only collect fresh young specimens as the older ones tend to be attacked by maggots. It has a fruity smell and tastes pleasant.

Collecting and Storing Suillus
Only pick fresh young mushrooms and cut off the earthy base before putting them in your basket.

Members of the *suillus* family are only suitable for drying and using as a flavouring. To preserve them you must first remove the gelatinous skin, but they are quite fiddly to peel. The best method is to clean the caps under running cold water, then place them on absorbent kitchen paper and leave to dry for 30 minutes. The skin will stick to the paper, so as you pull the paper away the skin will come with it.

Cut the caps and stalks into thin slivers and put on a baking sheet. Dry in a low oven or put the slices on a rack above a radiator and leave them to dry. Store in an airtight jar.

Uses
To flavour puréed soups, soak the dried slices in water for 20 minutes to soften, then add the mushrooms and their liquid with the stock.

Suillus variegatus

Slippery jack (*Suillus luteus*)

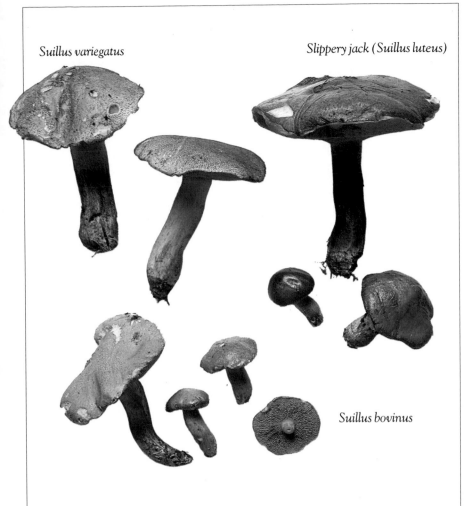

Suillus bovinus

Larch boletus (*Suillus grevilles*)

½ life size

They are delicious added to all vegetable soups, especially celeriac.
To flavour stews and sauces, grind these dried mushrooms to a powder and add them just before serving. Powdered *suillus* makes a tasty and unusual seasoning to sprinkle over the layers in gratin potatoes.

Caesar's Mushroom

Extreme care must be taken when gathering this mushroom because there are some deadly poisonous members in the *amanitas* group in which it belongs (see below). Caesar's mushroom (*Amanita caesarea*) is a very popular edible species in France. It does not grow in Britain, but favours deciduous woods in warm regions of Europe during the summer and early autumn.

It has a striking bright orange cap, measuring up to 18 cm (7 in) across, which fades yellow with age. The gills and club-shaped stem are yellow, and it has a drooping ring, which is easily detached. The base of the stalk is encased in a white sack known as a volva. This mushroom was the most highly prized edible species of Ancient Rome. It has a faint smell and tastes pleasant.

Two other members of the *amanitas* family are considered edible: the Blusher (*Amanita rubescens*) and Tawny Griselle (*Amanita fulva*). Both are common in deciduous and coniferous woods, but unless you are *totally* familiar with these mushrooms I would advise you to leave well alone, because they have three deadly poisonous relatives: the Death Cap (*Amanita phalliodes*), Panther Cap (*Amanita pantherina*) and the Destroying Angel (*Amanita virosa*), plus several others which make you seriously ill. It is this group of mushrooms which causes most cases of poisoning.

The whole *amanitas* family has certain characteristics to help you with identification: when very young they resemble an egg and are encased in a veil, which the buttons burst through; normally the cap is covered with flecks of veil remnant similar to tiny warts, but heavy rain can wash away the scaly patches. The stalk is encased by a volva, which may be loose and bag-like or only show as a rim around the base. Except for *Amanita caesarea* all members have white gills. The ones that are fatal to eat have a ring on the stem.

Collecting and storing

If you are travelling around the Mediterranean during the summer or autumn, you might be lucky and spot Caesar's mushroom growing in an oak wood, but do not confuse it with the red Fly Agaric (*Amanita muscaria*) which grows in Britain and is poisonous.

If you find a Caesar's mushroom, use a knife to dig out the whole fruiting body; be sure to collect the stem from under the ground so the volva can be seen. Take it to an expert or local pharmacy to have your identification confirmed; most French chemists have a display of edible fungi in their windows during the season, and they are only too pleased to help.

Use the mushrooms the day they are picked.

I cannot emphasize enough that extreme care must be taken when gathering any of the edible *Amanitas*. Do not eat any of them until you have had your identification confirmed – if you get it wrong, you may die.

Preparation and Cooking

Wipe mushroom caps and clean stalks thoroughly. Caesar's mushroom is delicious gently fried in olive oil with shallots. Just before serving, add a little crushed garlic and some finely chopped parsley.

Note: None of these mushrooms is illustrated.

Hedgehog fungus (Hydnum repandum)

²/₃ life size

Hedgehog Fungus

The Hedgehog Fungus (*Hydnum repandum*), also known as wood hedgehog, differs from all other edible fungi because instead of gills or pores it has spines, hence the common names. It is one of the easiest species to identify and there are no poisonous ones with a similar appearance to cause confusion.

The hedgehog fungus has a velvety creamy-apricot cap, 3-17 cm (1¼-6½ in) across, which becomes slightly funnel-shaped and tends to fold in on itself. In this form it can resemble a cloven hoof, hence the French name *pied de mouton*.

It is found in deciduous woods, usually in large numbers among brambles surrounding beech or oak trees, from late summer through to late autumn. Hedgehog fungus has a pleasant smell. Eaten raw it is rather bitter with a peppery aftertaste – this disappears with cooking. It is widely available in Europe.

If you happen to live in an area with sandy soil you might find its relative *Hydnam rufescens*, which has an orange to reddish cap. Although it does not grow in such profusion it is worth collecting.

Collecting and Storing

Hedgehog Fungus grows among leaf litter, and it is easy to pull the whole plant out of the ground gently. Once you have done this, cut away the earthy base of the stem and remove all the old leaves which have nestled in the cap before placing in your basket; the less dirt you take home the easier it is to clean them.

These mushrooms will keep in the refrigerator for 10 days. They are enjoyable to eat fresh during the autumn, but their mild flavour is not worth preserving for later use.

Preparation and Cooking

Wipe the caps with a damp cloth; if you were careful when you picked them, there should not be any soil trapped in the spines, but if there is, try and dislodge it with a small brush.

Hedgehog Fungi are rather dry and require slow cooking over a low heat. They are suitable for use in most mushroom recipes. Fried in butter, flavoured with fresh herbs and served on toast, they make a tasty snack. They are particularly good made into a sauce and served with chicken or game, or added to a fricassée.

Morel

Mushroom connoisseurs consider morels to be among the finest edible fungus, and fresh species are much sought-after in the spring, when they grow. They have become a rarity in Britain, but are abundant in most European countries, especially in France, where they are collected in vast quantities to be dried or canned. When fresh, they have a sweet, earthy smell and a slightly nutty taste.

MORCHELLA VULGARIS

The Common Morel (*Morchella vulgaris*) looks like a natural sponge on a stalk. The dome-shaped hollow cap is grey-brown turning a sandy colour with age, and the finely pitted surface resembles a honeycomb.

It is 5-12 cm (2-5½ in) tall. The cream, stocky stem is smooth. It can be found growing in rich soil in open woodland and gardens during late spring.

MORCHELLA ESCULENTA

Morchella esculenta is slightly taller than its cousin; the cap is 6-20 cm (2½-8 in) tall. The profile of the cap varies from bell-shaped to globular, and the honeycomb surface is camel-coloured, browning with age. The furrowed whitish stem is hollow like the cap.

This mushroom is difficult to find, and it is made even harder because people claim to have found it in various habitats. It is supposed to grow in rich chalky soil, under broad-leaved trees, hedgerows or in open parkland. Apparently it favours scorched ground and will appear on old bonfire tips. Old records reveal that these morels grew in groups on bomb sites in the war. Legend has it that in Germany during the 18th century peasant women would deliberately start forest fires to try and persuade them to grow.

The only place I have found these morels is under ash, growing among the moss and Dog's Mercury (a woodland weed). They are more common in southern England than northern counties, and can be found during late spring.

Europeans also enjoy eating the closely related *Morchella conica*, a small species with a dark grey cone-shaped cup; and *Morchella rotunda*, the largest member of the family, with a beige, spongy cap.

Collecting and Storing

If you are fortunate enough to find a colony of morels, cut off the earthy base before you put them in the basket, to avoid grit getting trapped in the pitted surface.

All morels are excellent for drying: thread the halved and cleaned mushrooms on a string and hang them above a radiator or in a warm kitchen for a couple of days. When they are dry and crisp, put them in an airtight jar. To reconstitute, soak them in water for 30 minutes.

If you cannot find any fresh species but would like to taste this mushroom, you can buy packets of dried morels from specialist delicatessens.

Preparation and Cooking

Cut each mushroom in half and wash carefully under running cold water to remove any dirt or insects which may be hiding in the crevices.

Morels should never be eaten raw because they are liable to cause nasty stomach upsets. In fact, it is preferable to blanch them for a few seconds prior to cooking.

Morels are exquisite prepared with cream and eaten on their own as a vegetable, or as a sauce with veal; add a few spoonfuls of Madeira and they are lovely served with chicken.

You can combine them with other species to make a soup and, like all mushrooms, they have an affinity with eggs; they are ideal to eat with scrambled eggs or you can add them to omelettes and flans.

Morel (*Morchella esculenta*)

²/₃ *life size*

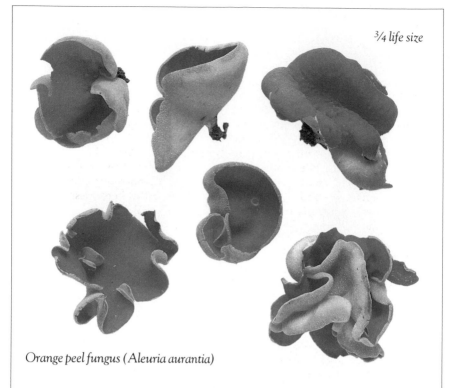

³/₄ *life size*

Orange peel fungus (Aleuria aurantia)

Orange Peel Fungus

A brightly coloured cup fungus, the Orange Peel Fungus (*Aleuria aurantia*), is very common. You usually find it growing in bare gravel, on paths, amongst grass in lawns or roadside verges, from early autumn until early winter.

It is cup shaped, becoming flattened and wavy with age, and it often has a split down one side. The inside of the cup is bright orange, but the outer surface is coated with a fine whitish down. The cup measures 1-10 cm (½-4 in) across.

Collecting and Storing
Use a knife to prize the mushroom out of the ground, and cut away the earthy base before putting them into your container to take home. I have never found orange peel fungus in large enough quantities to preserve, but it can be dried, although its beautiful colour fades to a rather dull brown.

Preparation and Cooking
Brush off any surface grit and wipe with a damp cloth. This fungus has an extremely mild delicate taste, hardly discernible, but it can be used to embellish other recipes. If you have only found a small number, cut them into thin slivers, otherwise use whole – their brilliant colour makes an attractive garnish for other mushroom dishes, soups, salads, or scattered over green vegetables – particularly broccoli – or mixed in with a French dressing.

Scarlet Elf Cap

A brilliant red cup fungus, Scarlet Elf Cap (*Sarcoscypha coccinea*) is quite rare in comparison to its cousin. It is found on dead wood, especially hazel or elm, during the winter and early spring and is quite common in the west of England. The inside of the cup is scarlet, while the outside looks as if it has been dusted with a fine white powder; it measures 1-5 cm (½-2 in) across. Apart from the obvious colour semblance, it is very similar to orange peel fungus (see above) and makes a striking garnish to adorn many savoury dishes.

Jew's Ear

This species can be found throughout the year, but is most prolific during the autumn. Jew's Ear (*Auricularia auricula judae*) is an ear-shaped bracket fungus, 3-8 cm (1¼-3¼ in) across, which grows in clusters and folds on dead branches of broad-leaved trees, especially elder. The name is supposed to refer to Judas, who reputedly hung himself on an elder tree. The upper surface is a soft, velvety, reddish-brown, whereas the inside is smooth, dull brown and feels like jelly. It turns dark brown with age and becomes rock hard.

This rather ugly fungus is a good edible, which is easy to identify. In China it is highly regarded, and related species, Wood Ear and Cloud Ear (see page 56), are cultivated, dried and sold in oriental grocers' stores throughout the world. They were also esteemed by herbalists, who added them to poultices to sooth sore eyes.

Collecting and Storing

Jew's ears should be gathered when they are young and soft. Use a knife to cut them from the tree. Separate the clusters and wash well under running cold water.

You can dry Jew's ears but they lack the flavour of their Chinese relatives. They will keep fresh in the refrigerator for 2 days.

Preparation and Cooking

Jew's ears need to be cooked slowly, because although they may feel soft they have a tendency to become leathery, especially if they are old. Slice into thin strips and stew them in milk for 40 minutes, then reduce the liquid and season with salt and plenty of ground pepper. Alternatively, simmer gently in butter with fresh herbs and serve on toast.

Jews' ears can be combined with other oriental species and used in most Chinese dishes, especially recipes including pork.

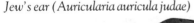

Jew's ear (Auricularia auricula judae)

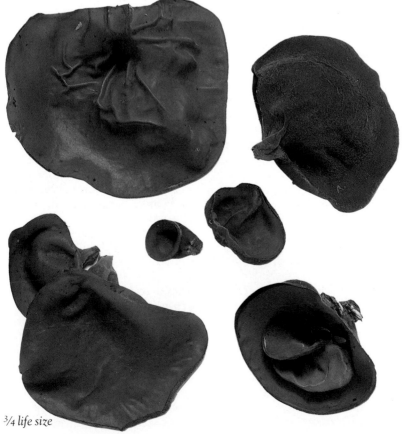

¾ life size

Beefsteak fungus (Fistulina hepatica)

½ life size

Beefsteak Fungus

The Beefsteak Fungus (*Fistulina hepatica*) is so called because the cut flesh looks like prime beef and a reddish juice seeps from the slices.

It is a bracket fungus which grows on the trunks of trees and its shape resembles a tongue, hence its other name 'Ox-tongue'.

The upper side is a reddish-orange which darkens as it matures to a purple-brown. The pores are pinkish-brown and bruise a dull red when touched. It can expand to as much as 30.5 cm (12 in) across. It grows on chestnut trees but is usually found on large oaks during late summer and autumn. It smells pleasant but has a rather sour taste when eaten raw.

This fungus causes brown rot in wood; oak acquires a darker, richer colour than normal when affected, and such timber is highly-prized among furniture makers, who refer to it as 'brown oak'.

Collecting and Storing
Use a knife to prize the beefsteak fungus away from the bark. Only collect small, tender specimens because as they develop they become tough and very bitter.

This bracket fungus will keep for 2 days in the refrigerator, but ideally it should be eaten as soon as possible because it has a tendency to dry out and become leathery.

Preparation and Cooking
This fungus prefers growing midway up an oak trunk; it is therefore usually very clean and only requires wiping with a moist cloth.

The best way to cook beefsteak fungus is to slice it into thin slivers and sauté slowly in butter with shallots, garlic and fresh herbs, especially thyme or marjoram, and seasoning, for about 20 minutes. The fungus exudes a vast quantity of juice, so it is necessary to increase the heat and reduce some of the liquid before serving.

Eat as an appetizer, with plenty of French bread to soak up the delicious sauce.

Dryad's Saddle

A large bracket fungus, Dryad's Saddle (*Polyporus squamosus*) is considered to be worth eating, but I have only found old fibrous ones which were tough and unpalatable. They can be found from late spring until early autumn, growing on deciduous trees, especially elm and beech.

Dryad's Saddle is usually fan-shaped and may be up to 60 cm (24 in) across.

These mushrooms tend to overlap one another. The fawny brown upper surface is speckled with darker scales, and the spores are cream. It has a strong mealy smell.

Note: This mushroom is not illustrated.

Chicken of the Woods

Chicken of the Woods (*Laetiporus sulphureus*) is a fleshy bracket fungus which grows in large tiers on old trees, especially oak, but can also be found on cherry, sweet chestnut and yew. It is found during spring and summer.

Chicken of the woods can range in colour from bright yellow to orange and fades to buff with age. It measures up to 40 cm (16 in) across and is irregularly fan-shaped or semi-circular. Its wrinkled surface feels like chamois leather. The young thick flesh exudes a lemon-coloured juice when squeezed, but as it dries out it will crumble.

This fungus is rarely eaten in Britain, possibly because it has only been tried when it is too old and has become sour, rancid and extremely leathery. However, in America chicken of the woods is considered a delicacy and it would appear high on their list of esteemed edible mushrooms. It is also popular in Germany.

It has a pleasant taste, a strong smell and fibrous meaty texture. It is often used as a substitute for chicken, hence its common name.

Collecting and Storing
Collect only young specimens by cutting them away from the tree bark. Unlike most fungus, chicken of the woods is suitable for freezing: cut into small cubes and either blanch or fry in butter before freezing. Alternatively store in the refrigerator for up to 2 days.

Preparation and Cooking
With young specimens, you can use virtually the whole bracket, except the woody centre core, but with the larger tiers only use the tender pale yellow frilly edge. Clean by wiping with a damp cloth and slice before cooking.

Chicken of the woods is wonderful added to chicken casseroles or made into a sauce; it will complement all chicken recipes and can even be used as a substitute.

Thin slivers sautéed in butter make an attractive garnish for soups and salads.

The simplest and possibly the most delicious way to cook this mushroom is to fry gently in butter with a finely chopped shallot and seasoning; just before they are cooked, add a generous squeeze of lemon juice. Serve alone or on toast for a light lunch. For an interesting starter add cream to this recipe, cook for a further 2 minutes and garnish with parsley.

⅓ life size

Chicken of the woods
(*Laetiporus sulphureus*)

Cauliflower Fungus

The Cauliflower Fungus (*Sparassis crispa*) resembles the heart of a cauliflower; some claim it looks rather more like brains, which is why it has also been christened 'brain fungus!'. You can occasionally find it growing at the base of conifer trees, particularly pines, during the autumn.

Cauliflower fungus bears a similar appearance in shape and colour to a natural sponge. This ochre fungus is easy to identify and can be as much as 50 cm (20 in) across. It discolours with age.

The young specimens have a slightly nutty taste and smell sweetish, but they become tough and bitter with age.

Few mushroom experts utilize this fungus because of its lengthy preparation, but once sampled you will enjoy its unique, delicate flavour. It rarely appears in shops. If you ever spot what you think to be this species, examine it carefully, because unless it is young and fresh it is not worth eating.

Collecting and Storing

Only pick young fresh specimens. If you are successful in finding a cauliflower fungus embedded in the roots of a pine, cut it off from the thick stem with a sharp knife. It is quite fragile, so put it in a basket rather than a carrier bag, to prevent it getting crushed on the way home.

This fungus is usually so vast that even if you give half of it away, there will be ample for several meals. It will keep fresh in the refrigerator for up to 10 days.

Cauliflower fungus is suitable for drying for later use as a flavouring for soups and stews. It also freezes well: you can blanch the flowerets, but it is preferable to sauté them gently in butter prior to freezing.

Preparation and Cooking

The only drawback with cauliflower fungus is that cleaning it is a laborious, time-consuming task – but do not let this deter you, because its delicious flavour is worth all the trouble. Start by removing all the pine needles, pieces of bracken and dead leaves which have been trapped in the frilly surface. Carefully break the cauliflower fungus into flowerets and cut away any brown edges or spongy parts. Rinse under running cold water to remove any grit or small insects which may be hiding in the folds; it is advisable to place a colander under the tap to catch the pieces which break off.

A simple way to cook cauliflower fungus is to dust the flowerets with flour and gently fry in butter for a few minutes; add seasoning, chives, parsley and thyme, and cook over a low heat to draw out the natural juices, which you then thicken with an egg yolk. Serve with a slice of lemon and chopped herbs to garnish. As an alternative, substitute spices for the herbs if you prefer a piquant flavour.

A more traditional way of preparing cauliflower fungus is to bake it in a casserole with butter, parsley, a finely chopped onion, a little garlic and some chicken stock.

Cauliflower fungus combines well with most rice recipes, and it makes an interesting addition to savoury fillings for tomatoes and marrows or for stuffed vine leaves. It can be used on its own or mixed with cultivated mushrooms.

The nutty flavour of this fungus makes it pleasant to eat raw, and the pale yellow flowerets look attractive tossed into a green salad or added to a shellfish dish. If you are lucky enough to find one early in the season, serve small pieces mixed in a dill vinaigrette with fresh crab.

¾ life size

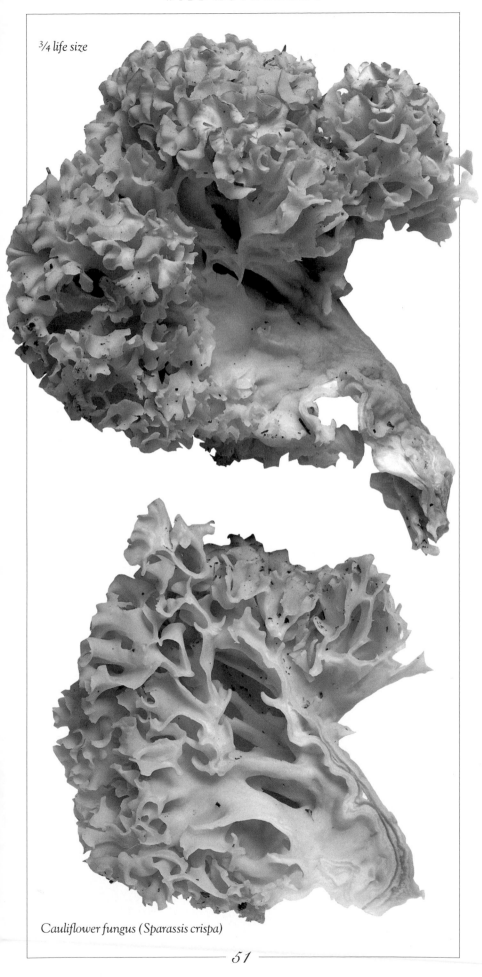

Cauliflower fungus (*Sparassis crispa*)

Giant Puff-ball

There is little point searching specifically for Giant Puff-balls (*Langermannia gigantea*) because you stumble across them nestling among a clump of nettles or tucked underneath a hedge, or you spot them from miles off glistening on a facing hillside or in a stubble field – looking like an abandoned football. In fact, you must try and resist the temptation to kick them!

Because of their immense size, with a girth that can expand to 70 cm (28 in), giant puff-balls are sometimes thought of as common, but you can go several years without seeing even one. They grow during late summer and early autumn. They are white when they first appear, but gradually fade to a dirty yellow, then brown when the leathery skin splits and they disintegrate.

Collecting and Storing

If you are lucky enough to spot giant puff-balls, collect only pure white ones. Try and keep each intact until you reach home, because it is fun to weigh and measure them – as you would prize vegetable marrows – and keep a record of size to compare with future finds.

A young specimen will keep in the refrigerator for 2 days. You can freeze puff-balls, but only do this if you have to, because they tend to become rather soggy when they are thawed. It is preferable to share your prize among friends and hope that you are fortunate enough to find another one next season.

Preparation and Cooking

Cut away the dirty base and wipe the surface with a damp cloth. There is no need to peel the kid-leather skin from a puff-ball – just cut it into slices, about 1 cm (½ in) thick. The flesh has a spongy texture similar to marshmallows.

A popular way to cook the slices is to dip them in an egg batter, then coat with toasted breadcrumbs and fry in bacon fat until golden brown – the crispness complements the flesh. Eat while hot for breakfast.

Alternatively, add a handful of chopped herbs to the batter, cook in olive oil with some garlic, and serve as a light lunch.

Giant puff-ball (Langermannia gigantea)

⅓ life size

Small puff-ball
(Lycoperdom pyriforme)

Small puff-ball
(Lycoperdom perlatum)

⅓ life size

Small Puff-balls

There are a lot of small puff-balls growing in Britain which are good to eat when they are white and tender. They look like miniature giant puff-balls. There are no poisonous species, but you must take care not to confuse them with earth-balls, which are not edible.

LYCOPERDON PERLATUM
This common puff-ball resembles a household light bulb in shape and grows up to 9 cm (3½ in) high. It is white at first, turning a dirty grey colour as it matures and finally a yellowish-brown. The flesh will also become powdery and disintegrate as it ages. It can be found in all types of woodland during late summer and autumn.

LYCOPERDOM PYRIFORME
A small pear-shaped puff-ball, with rough skin which feels similar to coarse sandpaper. It is whitish or light beige when young, darkening to a cinnamon brown with age. It grows to about 4 cm (1½ in) high and you usually find it in clusters on fallen trunks, old stumps or rotting wood. Although it might appear to be growing out of the earth, it will in fact be attached to a buried log. It is common from late summer and throughout the autumn.

VASCELLUM PRATENSE
This very common small puff-ball, cream in colour, is found growing on lawns, golf courses and pastures throughout the autumn.

Collecting and Preparing Small Puff-balls
Always collect young specimens. Cut away the earthy base to check that the flesh is pure white; if it has started to turn yellow, discard it. Most species have tough, scaly skin, so they need peeling before you use them.

They can be cooked like giant puff-balls (see opposite) or made into fritters by coating in a batter and deep-frying with a selection of vegetables.

Common White Helvella

The White Helvella (*Helvella crispa*) is a close relative of the morel. It can be found throughout the autumn and occasionally it also appears in the spring. It grows in moss and along the sides of paths in damp deciduous woods, especially near beech trees.

You can recognize this mushroom by its saddle-shaped cap, 2-5 cm (¾-2 in) high, which can be twisted and puckered like a piece of discarded paper. It is light cream with a pale buff or tan underside. The stem is hollow and deeply furrowed.

In a good year you might find as many as twenty growing in a line, but usually you only find two or three.

Another member of this family is the Black Helvella (*Helvella lacunosa*), which has a similar profile to its cousin, but the undulating cap is charcoal-grey, tinged with lilac, and sometimes it curls up to reveal the slightly paler underside. It can be found during the autumn in mixed woods, and it favours burnt ground.

Collecting and Storing

Pull the mushroom out of the moss and cut away the earthy base before you place it in your basket.

Helvellas will keep for 2 days in the refrigerator.

Preparation and Cooking

Wash under running cold water, making sure you get rid of any tiny insects which may lurk in the folds of the stem. This mushroom *must not* be eaten raw because it contains toxins which are only destroyed by cooking.

You can cook helvellas in similar ways to morels (see page 44) but they do not have the same distinctive flavour and they can be rather chewy.

As you are only likely to find helvellas in small quantities, serve as an appetizer. Dust them with flour and fry in butter with a clove of garlic, mixed herbs, seasoning and white wine; cook for 10 minutes or until the juices have reduced by half.

Common white helvella (*Helvella crispa*)

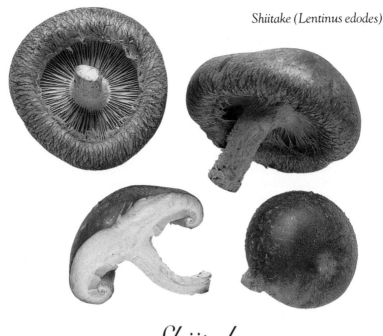

Shiitake (Lentinus edodes)

Shiitake

Shiitake (*Lentinus edodes*) were first grown by the Chinese, but it was the Japanese who developed methods of cultivating them. Traditionally they were grown on oak, teak or mahogany logs, but nowadays they use hardwood sawdust contained in a polythene mesh. They are farmed in Britain but most of the fresh shiitake for sale are imported from Holland, while the dried ones come from Japan.

The fresh caps are buff-brown, with a shaggy in-rolled margin and they feel similar to a chamois leather. Raw, they have a pronounced mushroomy taste with a slight peppery bite, which diminishes with cooking. In fact, fresh shiitake have a milder flavour than their dried counterparts.

Shiitake is the most common oriental dried mushroom sold in Britain. If you go into a Chinese supermarket and ask for dried fungus, you will most likely be given some shiitake.

Buying and Storing
Fresh shiitake are pre-packed in 250 g (8 oz) punnets and often sold in supermarkets. It is preferable to eat them within 1 or 2 days of purchase.

You can buy bags of the dried caps from Chinese grocery stores; these will keep for an indefinite period in an airtight container. Dried, they have a concentrated taste which is far more distinctive than fresh shiitake; therefore you only need 4 or 6 caps to flavour a recipe. They are delicious, and it is well worthwhile keeping a jar of them in the cupboard to add to clear soups, fricassées and stir-fries.

Preparation and Cooking
Shiitake have a slippery texture which is rather strange in Western recipes but is acceptable in Chinese and oriental dishes.

Whether preparing fresh or dried shiitake, discard the stalks because they are leathery. Remember, dried caps need to be soaked in water for 20 minutes to soften before you can cook with them. Add the mushroom liquid to the dish you are making, or save it for stock.

If you sauté these mushrooms, they absorb all the fat or oil and become rather greasy. It is better to stuff them with a savoury filling and bake. You can also blanch them and leave to cool, then toss into a green or mixed salad.

They are delicious cooked with chicken, in a clear soup or stir-fried; chicken and shiitake in a black bean sauce is wonderful. You can also steam them with white fish. A lovely way of serving shiitake is with a mixture of tempura vegetables and king prawns.

Wood Ear

A tree fungus, Wood Ear (*Auricularia polytricha*) is related to Jew's Ear (see page 47). The Chinese cultivate several varieties of this mushroom, ranging from 2.5-15 cm (1-6 in) across. There is a small, fragile species which is brownish-black on one side and grey-brown on the other; it is contorted and looks like a crumpled leaf. A larger member, which feels quite robust in comparison to its dainty friend, is charcoal-grey on top, with a buff underside which feels like suede. The gnarled clusters resemble clinker, which makes it hard to think of them as a great Chinese delicacy.

To add further confusion, this fungus is known by a variety of names: 'wood ear', 'cloud ear', 'silver ear' or 'dry black fungus'. You can buy packets of dried wood ears from oriental grocery stores.

The Chinese eat wood ears primarily for their unusual texture.

Preparation and Cooking
To reconstitute wood ears, soak in water for 30 minutes. As they begin to soften, separate the clusters so that any trapped dirt may fall to the bottom of the bowl. In fact, it is advisable to change the water several times to ensure that they are clean.

Only use a few clusters because they expand to about three times their original size. They turn brown, become rubbery like seaweed, have a mild taste and are extremely chewy. Thin slivers may be added to stir-fried or steamed dishes.

Padi-straw Mushroom

This species is popular in Southern China, South-East Asia and Madagascar. Padi-straw (*Volvariella volvacea*) or straw mushroom, as it is also called, is grown out of doors on rice straw. It has a greyish brown small cap. It is marketed fresh, dried or canned. It is difficult to find in Britain but you can buy it, canned, from specialist Chinese grocery stores and some supermarkets.

Padi-straw mushrooms can be stir-fried with beansprouts, young corns, spring onions and a few slices of fresh root (green) ginger, or added to steamed chicken recipes.

Matsutake

This species grows in pine forests in Japan, where it is considered a great delicacy. Matsutake (*Tricholoma matsutake*) is a large mushroom – the cap can measure up to 25 cm (10 in) in diameter.

It is occasionally imported canned into this country, but you will be extremely lucky if you can buy it. If you have a recipe which specifies matsutake, use its close relative, St. George's mushroom (*Tricholoma gambosum*) or Wood Blewit (*Lepista nuda*) as substitutes (see page 34-5), although they lack the exotic fragrance and taste.

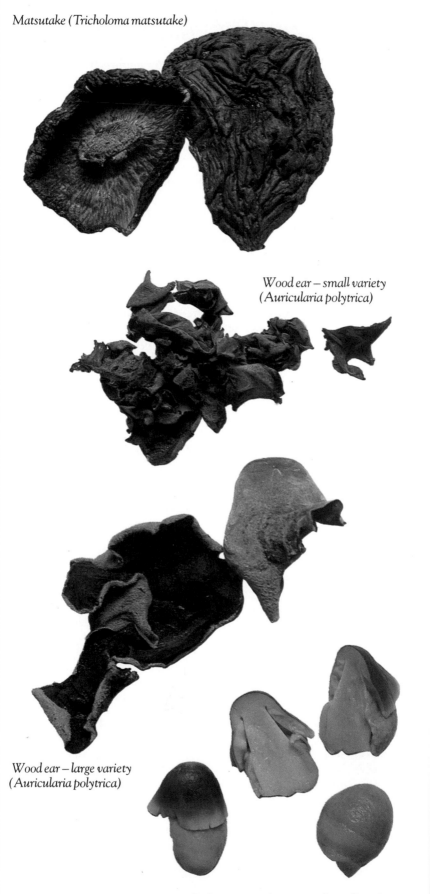

Matsutake (*Tricholoma matsutake*)

Wood ear – small variety
(*Auricularia polytrica*)

Wood ear – large variety
(*Auricularia polytrica*)

Padi-straw mushroom (*Volvariella volvacea*)

Cultivated Mushrooms

About half of the recipes in this book use cultivated mushrooms. Until comparatively recently mushrooms were a luxury food. Now everybody buys them – they are the most popular vegetable after the potato.

Mushroom cultivation was pioneered by the French in the mid-17th century. Traditionally mushrooms were grown in caves, but since the Second World War mushroom farms have proliferated and they are now grown in specially darkened buildings.

Farmed mushrooms (belonging to *Agaricus bisporus*, see page 12) are grown on elaborately mixed compost in wooden trays. The trays are pasteurized, then laboratory-prepared spores are sprinkled over the surface. Tiers of trays are placed in an incubating chamber until the mycelium – a thread-like mass which is the root system – covers the compost. The white 'cobweb' is coated with a layer of peat and chalk and the trays are then stacked in the growing houses. The first flush of mushrooms appears within 5 weeks. They are picked by hand; 4 or 5 crops are harvested from each tray.

These mushrooms are graded according to their size. **Buttons** are the small tightly closed white caps. Champignons de Paris are a particularly good variety of button mushrooms. **Cups** or **Open Cups**, as they are sometimes called, are slightly more mature with a stronger flavour. **Opens** or **Flats** are the big full-grown mushrooms with dark brown gills; they are compared to the wild field mushroom, possibly because of their richer flavour. Recently they have been marketed as 'breakfast mushrooms', presumably because they are delicious fried or grilled and served with bacon and eggs.

Farmers are also producing a brown-capped variety, **Chestnut** or **Marron**, which is claimed to have a fuller flavour than all the others.

The oyster mushroom (see page 30) is also now being cultivated.

Buying and Storing

Mushrooms are sold loose, or in pre-packed punnets. Whether buying loose or packaged, ensure mushrooms are fresh and firm with no blemishes.

Cultivated mushrooms are available all year at roughly the same price, so there is no need to freeze them. However, if you wish to do so, open-freeze them, then pack into containers, or freeze as a *duxelle* (see page 11).

Preparation and Cooking

Do not peel cultivated mushrooms, whatever the grade; simply trim the stalks and wipe them with a damp cloth to remove any dirt. To prevent discoloration after slicing, sprinkle with lemon juice.

The tiny buttons and cups are good to eat raw, tossed into salads, or as a crudité with other vegetables. They are also delicious sliced and mixed in a herb and lemon dressing, either on their own, or with avocado or bacon. Preserved in olive oil, with spices, garlic and black peppercorns, they will keep for several months in sealed jars; they are wonderful, and make attractive presents, especially at Christmas.

Cooked buttons, cups and chestnut mushrooms are ideal to add to soups such as Crab and Corn (see page 66) or Potato and Mushroom (see page 68). They can also be added to risottos or casseroles, or made into a sauce to be eaten with pasta. If the caps are firm enough, add to Prawn and Bacon Kebabs (see page 79).

The rich flavour of the open mushroom makes it a better ingredient for soups and stews. They can also be coated with a savoury butter or stuffed and baked. Flats are perfect to eat for breakfast.

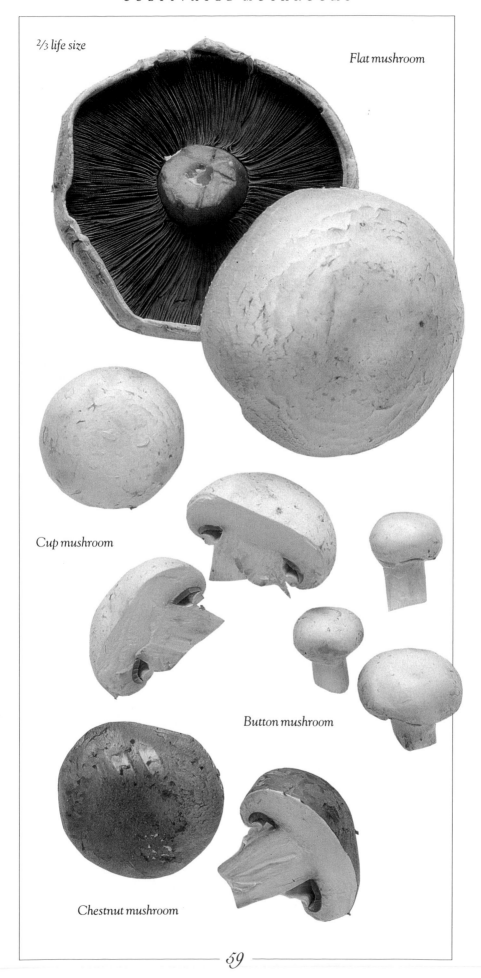

2/3 life size

Flat mushroom

Cup mushroom

Button mushroom

Chestnut mushroom

Truffles

There are three good edible species, which are highly prized for their intense flavour: the English or Summer Truffle, the Black French Truffle and the White Italian Truffle. The most coveted of these subterranean tubers is considered to be the one found in the Perigord district of France, although the Italians would probably dispute this claim!

There is an element of rivalry between the two countries, despite the fact that white and black truffles are totally different in taste and smell. That they are used in different ways also seems to be completely irrelevant. But both agree on one point: they dismiss the English truffle because it is smaller and supposedly has an inferior aroma.

The Italian or Piedmont truffle has a distinctive peppery taste and is usually eaten raw whereas the French and English truffles have a marvellous fragrance which pervades all other foods with which they come into contact; they are added to savoury dishes and sauces for their scent, but once they have been cooked they have very little flavour of their own.

Truffles are an expensive luxury. Good ones are distinguished by their fragrant aroma; they should feel light in proportion to their size, and 'give' slightly when squeezed. The best time to eat them is when they are fresh, because their perfume and flavour is considerably diminished by preserving.

The legendary tales suggesting that truffles are powerful aphrodisiacs are grossly exaggerated, although they do stimulate the appetite and aid digestion.

Truffles are supposed to favour well drained ground beneath deciduous trees, especially oaks. They grow in small clusters 10-20 cm (4-8 in) below the soil, and they do not venture beyond the leaf canopy. Most of the Perigord truffles are found in oak plantations, where they grow spontaneously – they were not planted, they just arrived.

In France they have been trying to cultivate truffles: young oaks have been impregnated with the spores and mycelium has been planted at the base of the trees to try and increase production, but so far no satisfactory method of cultivating truffles has been found.

TRUFFLE HUNTING

It is extremely difficult – and requires endless patience – to find truffles without animals. Nowadays nobody in Britain seems to gather them, or if they do, they are extremely secretive about their forays. In France the harvest is carried out in a haphazard manner; the detective work is done mainly by pigs, who have an insatiable appetite for truffles, which maybe explains why they are inclined to eat their precious find! The pungent odour includes a phenomenon which is similar to that given off by pigs when they are in season; this is why they are able to sniff them out and then grub them up with their snouts. Because of the difficulties the French have in controlling their swine, they are now training and using dogs to scent out their truffles – the Italian way.

Although dogs do not have such a sensitive nose for these tubers, they are reliable and do not tire as quickly as pigs. They have to be carefully looked after to avoid spoiling their noses. Young dogs are coupled to old hounds and a truffle is rubbed on their noses to give them the scent. The dogs locate the truffles and their masters help dig.

A possible alternative way of locating truffles is to find a potential site and look out for a cloud of flies hovering just above the ground, or search for animal scratchings, especially where badgers and squirrels have rooted, because they, like the flies, will have been lured by the aroma from the developing tubers. It is worth continuing the excavations of the woodland population because you might be lucky and find a truffle buried beneath the leaf litter.

Summer truffle (Tuber aestivum)

Summer Truffle

The Summer or English Truffle (*Tuber aestivum*), also known as the 'Bath truffle', has become a rarity. It used to be found in the southern counties of England, especially on the Downs in Hampshire, Wiltshire and Kent. It is blue-black with a warty skin and can be distinguished from its French twin by its marbled beige-white flesh. It varies in size from 3-7 cm (1¼-2½ in) across.

English truffles have a sweet scent and nutty taste. In season from late summer to autumn, they grow in light, dry chalky soil and seem to favour beech trees to oaks.

There used to be a thriving truffle trade in England – Spanish poodles were used to sniff them out of beech forests. The last documents about professional truffle-hunting record the activities of Alfred Colins who, with two dogs, scoured the woods near his home in Winterslow, in Wiltshire. After a long day's exertion, he would carry his dogs home on his bicycle in specially made leather panniers.

Sadly the summer truffle seems to have all but vanished, but I am sure there are some beneath the soil; it is not the truffles that have disappeared but those who know how to find them.

You cannot buy summer truffles. The ones illustrated were found in Gloucestershire by a friend who lent them to me to photograph. As they had to be returned the next day, I kept some in a jar of rice and some in the refrigerator by the butter. The rice smelt and tasted wonderful in a simple risotto. I appreciated the savoury butter on some hot toast and realized I was eating what might be called 'Poor man's truffle' – it was a delicious treat with which to start the day.

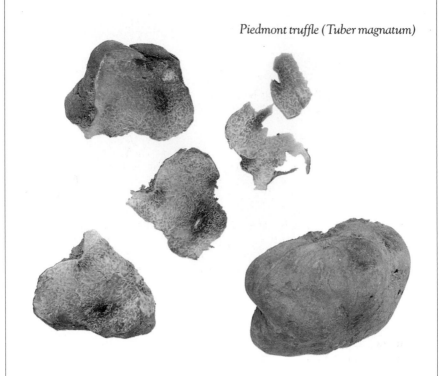

Piedmont truffle (Tuber magnatum)

Piedmont Truffle

The Piedmont Truffle (*Tuber magnatum*) is also called the 'white truffle' probably to distinguish it from the black tubers, because in reality it is a dirty-brown colour outside and beige inside. These truffles are found in northern Italy – in Tuscany, Romagna and Piedmont, where the finest ones grow. The Italians use specially trained dogs to hunt them out. The season extends from late autumn until early spring. Piedmont truffles are usually the size of bantam eggs, but specimens as large as tennis balls may be found.

Buying and Storing
Fresh white truffles can be bought in Italian markets in season but they are extremely difficult to buy in Britain unless you happen to know of a specialist importer or friendly restaurateur who would be willing to part with one.

If you are unable to locate a fresh supply, the canned or bottled ones are well worth sampling. Whether it's their delicate flavour and scent, or their scarcity value, these truffles are the most expensive variety to

buy and should be used sparingly. If you can afford a fresh white truffle, it can be stored overnight in the refrigerator with some fresh spaghetti, or put into a jar with some dry tagliatelle to flavour the pasta.

Preparation and Cooking
Brush away the surface dirt and wipe with a damp cloth if necessary. These truffles are not usually cooked because high temperatures can spoil the flavour and they lose their magic aroma. If required, heat them gently with a little butter.

Scatter paper-thin slices over plain pasta dishes or simple risottos, or place on top of a Piedmont cheese fondue. Like their peers, they have an affinity with eggs, and shavings are delicious sprinkled over scrambled eggs or omelettes; the Italians grate them over fried eggs.

Add slivers to the anchovy, garlic and oil sauce *bagna cauda* and serve with crudités. Another popular method of serving truffles is with chicken or turkey breasts and cheese. You can also use them to garnish thin veal escalopes.

Perigord Truffle

There are a few peasant farmers in France who adhere to the old traditions and go truffle-hunting with pigs, but most French people use trained dogs. The finest truffles are gathered from around Perigord and Magny.

The Perigord or Black truffle (*Tuber melanosporum*) has a rough bluish-black skin which turns brownish with age. The cut flesh turns a violet-black and is covered by a fine network of whitish veins. Their shape and size can vary from that of a walnut to a fist, and they have a penetrating sweet aroma.

Buying and Storing

In France, fragrant black truffles are available during the autumn and early winter. They are sometimes imported into Britain.

They should feel softish to the touch and have a perfumed aroma. If you cannot find fresh ones, they are obtainable canned or bottled.

These expensive tubers only keep for a week, but you can extend their use and flavour: place one in the middle of a bowl of eggs – their scent will penetrate the shells by the next day and the eggs will taste delicious; add one or two black truffles to a jar of rice or put in the refrigerator next to some butter or any other food of your choice – their exotic odour is extremely pervasive.

Preparation and Cooking

To clean a Perigord truffle, remove all the surface dirt, which is embedded in its knobbly skin, with a soft brush, or wash under running cold water if necessary.

Cooking them whole in champagne or wine is sheer extravagance. They are perfect used as a flavouring for stuffings, game or duck pâté; the French add them to *foie gras*. Canned truffles are not really suitable to use in pâtés, because their delicate flavour tends to be lost. When you use preserved truffles, remember to add the juice to the recipe.

Black truffles have an affinity with eggs. Tiny pieces can be mixed in with scrambled eggs or used to season soufflés. Thin slivers are lovely as a topping for eggs en cocotte, or sprinkled over an omelette which has been enriched with cream and madeira.

A traditional delicacy is chicken or turkey flavoured with truffles: thin slices of truffle are placed under the skin of the uncooked bird, which is left overnight to allow the flavour to penetrate the flesh before it is filled with stuffing and roasted.

A crafty ploy that the French use to eke out the appearance of their truffles is to mix them with finely chopped Horn of Plenty (see page 20). You can use the mixture to stuff a roast pork tenderloin.

Perigord truffle
(Tuber melanosporum)

Cream of Mushroom Soup

750 g (1½ lb) mushrooms (see note)
45 g (1½ oz) butter
1 shallot, finely chopped
½ clove garlic, chopped
15 g (½ oz/6 teaspoons) plain flour
125 ml (4 fl oz/½ cup) white wine
785 ml (25 fl oz/3 cups) stock (see note)
125 ml (4 fl oz/½ cup) double (thick) cream
salt and pepper, to taste
TO GARNISH:
4 tablespoons double (thick) cream
sprigs of parsley

Prepare mushrooms according to their type and chop roughly. In a large saucepan, melt butter, add mushrooms, shallot and garlic and cook for a few minutes, stirring. Stir in flour and cook for 1 minute. Add wine and stock, a little at a time, stirring well between each addition.

Bring to the boil, then cover and simmer for 20 minutes.

In a food processor or blender, purée the soup, in batches if necessary, and return to pan. Over a gentle heat, stir in cream, and salt and pepper.

Transfer to warmed soup bowls, swirl a spoonful of cream on top and garnish with parsley.

Serves 4.

Note: Button mushrooms give a good colour to this soup; if they are available, include some wild mushrooms too, for their superior flavours. Fairy rings, morels, champignons de Paris, field and horse mushrooms are good choices.

Use mushroom stock for this soup if possible; otherwise use vegetable or chicken stock.

Carrot Soup with Croûtons

30 g (1 oz) butter

1 small onion, finely chopped

500 g (1 lb) carrots, sliced

5 cm (2 in) piece fresh root (green) ginger, chopped

940 ml (30 fl oz/3¾ cups) chicken stock

1 bay leaf

pinch of freshly grated nutmeg

90 ml (3 fl oz/⅓ cup) double (thick) cream

3 tablespoons brandy

salt and pepper, to taste

MUSHROOM CROÛTONS:

60 g (2 oz) butter, softened

90 g (3 oz) mushrooms, finely chopped

2 teaspoons finely chopped parsley

½ small clove garlic, crushed

8 slices French bread

TO GARNISH:

sprigs of coriander or parsley

In a large saucepan, melt butter, add onion and sauté for 2 minutes, to soften. Add carrots and ginger and cook for 2-3 minutes. Pour in stock and bring to the boil; add bay leaf and nutmeg. Cover and simmer for 20-25 minutes, until carrots are soft.

In a food processor or blender, purée the soup, in batches if necessary, and return to pan. Over a gentle heat, stir in cream, brandy, and salt and pepper.

To make croûtons, in a small bowl mix together butter, mushrooms, parsley and garlic. Toast bread on one side only; turn and spread the other side with mushroom butter. Just before serving, return croûtons to the grill until hot and golden.

Serve soup in warmed bowls. Float 2 croûtons on each and garnish with coriander or parsley.

Serves 4.

Note: The soup may be prepared in advance and the croûtons spread with mushroom butter ready for toasting at the last minute.

Crab, Corn & Mushroom Soup

940 ml (30 fl oz/3¾ cups) chicken stock

2.5 cm (1 in) piece fresh root (green) ginger, roughly chopped

2 spring onions, roughly chopped

185 g (6 oz) cooked sweetcorn kernels

3 tablespoons groundnut oil

125 g (4 oz) button mushrooms, quartered

185 g (6 oz) white crab meat, in small pieces

2 eggs, lightly beaten

salt and pepper, to taste

TO GARNISH:

coriander leaves

Put stock, ginger and spring onions in a saucepan. Bring to the boil, then cover and simmer for 15 minutes.

Meanwhile, in a food processor or blender, work half of the sweet-corn kernels to a smooth purée.

Strain the stock and discard the flavourings.

In the same pan, heat oil, add mushrooms and sauté for 2 minutes, to soften. Stir in remaining sweet-corn kernels, sweetcorn purée and stock. Bring to the boil, then simmer for 10 minutes.

Just before serving, stir in crab meat and bring to a gentle simmer. Pour in beaten eggs, in a slow stream, stirring constantly; check seasoning.

Serve in warmed soup bowls, garnished with coriander.

Serves 4.

Note: This soup may be prepared in advance up to the stage before the crab is added.

Chicken Soup Chinese-style

5 dried shiitake mushrooms
785 ml (25 fl oz/3 cups) well-flavoured chicken stock
2 slices plus ¼ teaspoon finely chopped fresh root (green) ginger
2 sprigs of coriander
10 cm (4 in) piece lemon grass
pinch of sugar
2 spring onions, shredded
2 teaspoons soy sauce
2 tablespoons dry sherry or rice wine
125 g (4 oz) cooked chicken, in small strips
Szechuan pepper, to taste

Put dried shiitake mushrooms in a small bowl, cover with warm water and leave to soak for 20 minutes; strain, reserving soaking liquor. Rinse shiitakes thoroughly, trim stalks and slice.

Put stock, mushroom liquor, sliced ginger, coriander, lemon grass and sugar in a saucepan. Bring to the boil, then cover and simmer for 30 minutes. Strain through a fine sieve, discarding flavourings. Return stock to the pan and add the mushrooms and remaining ingredients. Bring to the boil, cover and simmer for 10 minutes. Check seasoning and serve, piping hot.

Serves 4.

Potato & Mushroom Soup

45 g (1½ oz) butter

1 onion, chopped

750 g (1½ lb) potatoes, cut into 1 cm (½ in) dice

2 bacon rashers, rinds removed, diced

375 g (12 oz) chestnut mushrooms, quartered

940 ml (30 fl oz/3¾ cups) bacon stock

315 ml (10 fl oz/1¼ cups) creamy milk

freshly grated nutmeg

salt and pepper, to taste

TO GARNISH:

grilled bacon, crumbled

snipped chives

In a saucepan, melt butter, add onion and sauté gently for 4-5 minutes, until pale golden. Stir in potato, bacon and mushrooms and cook for 1 minute. Add stock, milk and a sprinkling of nutmeg. Bring to the boil, cover and simmer for 20 minutes, skimming occasionally.

In a food processor or blender, purée half the soup mixture; return to remainder in pan. Season with salt and pepper.

Serve hot, garnished with bacon and chives.

Serves 6.

Smoked Salmon Pâté

280 g (9 oz) smoked salmon slices
75 g (2½ oz) butter
280 g (9 oz) button mushrooms
75 g (2½ oz) fromage fraîs
1½ teaspoons lemon juice
2 teaspoons chopped chervil
salt and pepper, to taste
TO GARNISH:
sprigs of chervil
lemon slices

Use 185 g (6 oz) smoked salmon to line the base and side of four 125 ml (4 fl oz/½ cup) ramekins. Set aside. Roughly chop remaining smoked salmon.

In a saucepan, melt butter, add mushrooms and sauté for about 5 minutes, until soft. Transfer to a food processor or blender and allow to cool. Add chopped smoked salmon and purée until smooth. Transfer to a bowl and fold in fromage fraîs, lemon juice and chervil. Season with salt and pepper.

Divide pâté between prepared ramekins, folding over any overlapping salmon. Cover each ramekin with plastic wrap and chill for at least 1 hour.

To serve, turn out salmon-wrapped pâté onto serving plates and garnish with chervil and lemon slices. Serve with melba toast.

Serves 4.

Oyster Mushroom Beignets

500 g (1 lb) oyster mushrooms
oil for deep-frying
BEER BATTER:
125 g (4 oz/1 cup) plain flour
½ teaspoon salt
2 eggs, separated
155 ml (5 fl oz/⅔ cup) beer
2 tablespoons olive oil
DIP:
155 ml (5 fl oz/⅔ cup) thick sour cream
1 tablespoon lemon juice
½ clove garlic, crushed
1 teaspoon clear honey
4 tablespoons finely chopped lemon balm
salt and pepper, to taste
TO GARNISH:
sprigs of lemon balm

First prepare batter: sift flour and salt into a bowl, add egg yolks, then gradually whisk in beer to form a smooth batter. Stir in oil and set aside.

Mix all ingredients for dip together in a small bowl.

Heat oil to 180C (350F). In a bowl, whisk egg whites until soft peaks form, then fold into batter mixture. Dip mushrooms into batter and deep-fry, in batches, in hot oil for about 2 minutes, until crisp and golden. Drain on absorbent kitchen paper and keep hot while frying remaining mushrooms.

Serve the mushroom beignets with the dip, garnished with lemon balm.

Serves 4.

Variation: Use small cup mushrooms or chanterelles in place of oyster mushrooms.

Bagna Cauda

315 ml (10 fl oz/ 1 ¼ cups) whipping cream
3 cloves garlic, crushed
2 x 50 g (1 ¾ oz) cans anchovy fillets, drained and chopped
60 g (2 oz) unsalted butter, cut into pieces
TO GARNISH:
sprigs of parsley
TO SERVE:
whole button mushrooms
radishes
cubes of crusty bread

Put cream, garlic and anchovy fillets in a small saucepan, bring to the boil, then simmer gently, uncovered, for 12-15 minutes, until smooth and thickened. Stir in butter.

Transfer to a serving dish and garnish with parsley. Serve with mushrooms, radishes and cubes of bread for dipping.

Serves 4.

Note: This dish originates from the Piemonte region of north-west Italy where it was traditionally served as a dip for 'cardoon', a locally grown edible thistle. I think it is superb with firm white button mushrooms. Keep the dip hot at the table over a candle or spirit burner.

Marinated Flat Mushrooms

6 tablespoons virgin olive oil

1 teaspoon coriander seeds, lightly crushed

½ teaspoon ground bay leaf

500 g (1 lb) flat mushrooms

finely grated rind of ½ lime

juice of 1 lime

1 clove garlic, crushed

2 tablespoons white wine or cider vinegar

pinch of sugar

salt and pepper, to taste

TO GARNISH:

1 tablespoon chopped parsley

lime slices

sprigs of parsley

In a large saucepan, heat 3 tablespoons olive oil, add coriander seeds and cook for 1 minute. Stir in ground bay leaf and mushrooms and cook over low heat for 5-7 minutes, until mushrooms are just tender. Remove from heat and add remaining ingredients, mixing well.

Transfer to a shallow bowl and allow to cool, then cover and chill for at least 2 hours.

Check seasoning, sprinkle with chopped parsley and garnish with lime and parsley sprigs. Serve with crusty French bread.

Serves 4.

Variation: Substitute fennel seeds for coriander seeds to give a hint of aniseed flavour.

Whole button mushrooms could be used in place of flat ones.

Quail's Eggs on a Nest

90 g (3 oz) curly endive

4 tablespoons walnut oil

½ clove garlic, crushed

4 large flat mushrooms

12 quail's eggs

3 streaky bacon rashers, rinds
removed, cut into small strips

5 teaspoons white wine vinegar

salt and pepper, to taste

2 teaspoons snipped chives

TO GARNISH:

few chives

Arrange endive on individual serving plates; set aside. In a large non-stick frying pan, heat 2 tablespoons oil, add garlic and mush-rooms and cook for 2 minutes or until mushrooms are just tender. Place stalk side up on top of endive.

Add remaining oil to pan and fry quail's eggs, in 4 batches, for about 30 seconds; carefully transfer them to the mushrooms.

Add bacon to pan and cook over high heat until crisp. Add vinegar and heat, scraping up all the bacon juices; season with salt and pepper.

Pour hot dressing over the endive and sprinkle 'nests' with chives. Serve immediately, garnished with chives.

Serves 4.

Morels and Oysters in Brioche

4 brioches

185 g (6 oz) fresh morels

60 g (2 oz) butter

½ small onion, finely chopped

60 ml (2 fl oz/¼ cup) dry white wine

185 ml (6 fl oz/¾ cup) double (thick) cream

6 freshly shucked oysters, halved

1 teaspoon arrowroot, blended with 2 teaspoons water

2-3 teaspoons lemon juice

salt and pepper, to taste

TO GARNISH:

mixed salad leaves

Preheat oven to 160C (325F/Gas 3).

Slice the tops from the brioches and hollow out the inner crumbs. Put brioches and tops on a baking sheet and set aside.

To prepare morels, slice in half down the centre and put in a bowl of salted water. Leave to soak for 15 minutes, then rinse carefully. Blanch in boiling water for 2 minutes; drain.

In a saucepan, melt butter, add onion and sauté for 2 minutes. Stir in wine and mushrooms and cook over high heat, until almost all the liquid has evaporated. Add cream and oysters and heat gently until almost boiling. Stir in blended arrowroot and cook, stirring, until thickened. Add lemon juice to taste and season with salt and pepper.

Divide mixture between the brioches. Replace lids and bake in the oven for 15-20 minutes or until hot. Serve immediately, with salad leaves to garnish.

Serves 4.

Variation: Cultivated mushrooms can be used in place of morels. Cut into quarters or slices and add to butter as above.

Chèvre & Mushroom Croustades

155 g (5 oz) wild mushrooms (see note)
1-2 teaspoons sesame oil
30 g (1 oz) butter
125 g (4 oz/2 cups) soft white breadcrumbs
4-5 teaspoons sesame seeds
185 g (6 oz) soft chèvre (goat's cheese)
3 teaspoons finely chopped sun-dried tomato (see note)
3 teaspoons chopped basil
1 tablespoon virgin olive oil
TO GARNISH:
basil leaves
salad leaves

Preheat oven to 200C (400F/Gas 6). Prepare mushrooms according to type, chopping roughly unless very small; set aside. Brush four 7-10 cm (3-4 in) tartlet tins with sesame oil.

In a small saucepan, melt butter and stir in breadcrumbs and 3 teaspoon sesame seeds. Divide between tartlet tins, pressing onto side, and bake in the oven for 12-15 minutes, until pale golden and crisp.

Meanwhile, in a small bowl, mix together chèvre, sun-dried tomato and basil; set aside.

In a small frying pan, heat olive oil, add mushrooms and sauté for 1 minute. Reserve a few mushrooms for garnish and divide the rest between the cooked croustade shells. Top with the chèvre mixture, spreading to fill the shells. Top with reserved mushrooms and sprinkle with remaining sesame seeds. Return to the oven for 10 minutes, until hot.

Serve hot or warm, garnished with basil and salad leaves.

Serves 4.

Note: Use chanterelles, fairy rings, champignons de Paris, ceps or oyster mushrooms, or a mixture of fresh wild mushrooms, if you can get them; sliced button mushrooms can be substituted if not.

Sun-dried tomatoes are available in jars, preserved in olive oil, from many delicatessens and specialist food shops.

Ravioli with Three Cheeses

EGG PASTA:

125 g (4 oz/1 cup) plain flour
1 large egg
1 teaspoon olive oil
pinch of salt

FILLING:

15 g (1 oz) dried ceps (porcini)
90 g (3 oz) ricotta cheese
90 g (3 oz) smoked mozzarella cheese, finely chopped
2 tablespoons double (thick) cream
pepper, to taste
12 flat parsley leaves

TO SERVE:

30 g (1 oz) butter, melted
1-2 tablespoons freshly grated Parmesan cheese

To make the pasta dough, sift flour onto a work surface. Make a well in the centre and add egg, oil and salt. Gradually work flour into egg mixture and knead together, adding a little water if the dough seems dry. Lightly dust the work surface with flour and knead the dough firmly for at least 5 minutes, until smooth and elastic. Wrap in plastic wrap and set aside for 1 hour.

Meanwhile, put ceps in a small bowl, cover with warm water and leave to soak for 20 minutes. Rinse thoroughly to remove any grit, drain well and chop roughly.

To make filling, mix together cheeses, cream, ceps and pepper.

On a lightly floured surface, roll out dough until it is paper-thin; cut into 24 squares. Divide filling between 12 squares and place a parsley leaf on each; cover with remaining pasta squares. (The parsley should be visible through the thin pasta.) Press the edges of each ravioli to seal, trim to neaten squares and crimp the edges with a fork. Leave for 10 minutes to dry slightly before cooking.

Cook in a large saucepan of boiling salted water for 3 minutes; drain well. Serve 3 ravioli per person. Drizzle with melted butter and sprinkle with Parmesan. Accompany with a little dressed radicchio salad.

Serves 4.

Gruyère & Mushroom Tart

PASTRY:
185 g (6 oz/1½ cups) plain flour
pinch of salt
125 g (4 oz) butter, cut into pieces
1 egg yolk
FILLING:
15 g (½ oz) butter
1 shallot, finely chopped
185 g (6 oz) mushrooms, chopped (see note)
125 g (4 oz) gruyère cheese, grated
3 eggs, lightly beaten
250 ml (8 fl oz/1 cup) whipping cream
pepper, to taste
good pinch of freshly grated nutmeg

Preheat oven to 220C (425F/Gas 7).

To make pastry, sift flour and salt into a large bowl and rub in butter until mixture resembles breadcrumbs. Add egg yolk and 2-3 tablespoons water and mix to a firm but pliable dough. On a lightly floured surface, roll out pastry and use to line a 20 cm (8 in) flan ring; chill for 15 minutes. Bake blind in the oven for 15 minutes. Lower temperature to 190C (375F/Gas 5).

Meanwhile, prepare filling. In a small saucepan, melt butter, add shallot and sauté for 4-5 minutes, stirring, until golden. Add mushrooms and cook for 2-3 minutes, until softened. Transfer to prepared pastry case.

In a bowl, mix together cheese, eggs and cream; season with pepper. Pour into pastry case and sprinkle with nutmeg. Bake in the oven for about 35 minutes, until the filling is just set. Serve warm, cut into wedges, with salad.

Serves 6.

Note: Use any mushroom variety for this recipe, or a mixture. Dried mushrooms can be used to give a good flavour: try morels, ceps (porcini), or the inexpensive blend, Mélanges Forestière. Use 30 g (1 oz) dried weight, soak in warm water for 20 minutes and rinse well.

Mussel Stuffed Crêpes

155 ml (5 fl oz/²/₃ cup) dry white wine
1 clove garlic, crushed
1 shallot, finely chopped
1 kg (2 lb) mussels, cleaned
8 crêpes
TOMATO SAUCE:
1 tablespoon olive oil
1 small onion, chopped
500 g (1 lb) tomatoes, chopped
pinch of sugar
2 teaspoons chopped parsley
salt and pepper, to taste
FILLING:
30 g (1 oz) butter
1 shallot, chopped
185 g (6 oz) wild mushrooms, chopped
6 tablespoons crème fraîche
2 teaspoons chopped parsley

Preheat oven to 190C (375F/Gas 5).

Put wine, garlic, shallot and 90 ml (3 fl oz/¹/₃ cup) water in a large pan. Add mussels, cover and cook over high heat for 3-5 minutes, until opened; discard any unopened ones. Strain, retaining cooking liquor. Remove mussels from shells, leave a few unshelled for garnish; set aside.

To prepare tomato sauce, in a saucepan, heat oil and sauté onion over low heat for 4-5 minutes. Add tomatoes, reserved mussel liquor and sugar, cover and cook for 5 minutes. Remove from heat and stir in parsley. Purée in a food processor or blender, then sieve. Return to pan and cook until reduced and thick; season with salt and pepper.

For the filling, melt butter in a frying pan and sauté shallot for 2 minutes. Stir in mushrooms and cook for 2-3 minutes, until tender. Off the heat, stir in mussels, crème fraîche and parsley; check seasoning.

Divide filling between crêpes and fold into quarters. Arrange in one layer in a buttered ovenproof dish and heat in oven for 15 minutes.

Reheat tomato sauce. Garnish crêpes with mussels and serve with tomato sauce.

Serves 4.

Note: Use parasols, chanterelles, morels, fairy rings, ceps or field mushrooms for optimum flavour.

Prawn & Bacon Kebabs

12 cooked king prawns, deveined and halved crosswise
12 streaky bacon rashers, rinds removed, halved
walnut oil, for brushing
MUSHROOM & RICE BALLS:
15 g (½ oz) butter
3 teaspoons walnut oil
1 shallot, finely chopped
1 clove garlic, crushed
125 g (4 oz) button mushrooms, finely chopped
185 g (6 oz) long-grain rice, cooked
75 g (2½ oz) fresh white breadcrumbs
4 teaspoons chopped coriander leaves
1 egg, beaten
salt and pepper, to taste
TO GARNISH:
salad leaves

First make mushroom and rice balls: in a saucepan, heat butter and walnut oil, add shallot and garlic and cook for 1 minute, to soften. Stir in mushrooms, rice, breadcrumbs, coriander and egg; season with salt and pepper. Preheat grill to hot. Shape mixture into 16 walnut-sized balls, put on a baking sheet and cook under the hot grill for 3 minutes, turning once, until firm.

Wrap each piece of king prawn in half a rasher of bacon. Thread bacon-wrapped prawns and mushroom and rice balls alternately on 8 short skewers. Put on a baking sheet and brush with walnut oil. Cook under the hot grill for 5 minutes, turning occasionally, until bacon is cooked and lightly browned.

Garnish kebabs with salad leaves to serve.

Serves 4.

Lemon Sole with Mushrooms

8 small fillets lemon sole, skinned

315 ml (10 fl oz/1¼ cups) fish or chicken stock

315 ml (10 fl oz/1¼ cups) dry white wine

2 teaspoons arrowroot, blended with a little water

4 tablespoons double (thick) cream

1 tablespoon chopped fennel leaves

salt and pepper, to taste

STUFFING:

30 g (1 oz) butter

4 tablespoons finely chopped fennel bulb

250 g (8 oz) oyster mushrooms, chopped

45 g (1½ oz) pine kernels, toasted and chopped

60 g (2 oz/1 cup) fresh white breadcrumbs

grated rind and juice of ½ lemon

TO GARNISH:

few oyster mushrooms, cooked

fennel leaves

2 teaspoons pine kernels, toasted

Preheat oven to 190C (375F/Gas 5).

First prepare stuffing: in a saucepan, melt butter, add chopped fennel bulb and sauté for 1 minute, to soften. Add mushrooms and cook for 2-3 minutes, until tender. Stir in pine kernels, breadcrumbs, lemon rind and juice.

Lay fish fillets flat, skinned side up. Divide stuffing between them and roll up. Place seam side down in a shallow ovenproof dish. Mix stock and wine together and pour over fish. Cover loosely with foil and bake in the oven for 25 minutes, until cooked. Carefully transfer fish fillets to a plate and keep warm. Reserve cooking juices.

Strain the fish juices into a small saucepan, bring to the boil and reduce by half. Stir in blended arrowroot and cook, stirring, until thickened; remove from heat and stir in cream and chopped fennel leaves. Season with salt and pepper.

Arrange fish on warmed serving plates and pour sauce over and around. Garnish with whole mushrooms, fennel leaves and pine nuts. Serve with wild rice.

Serves 4.

Salmon with Mushrooms & Dill

4 salmon steaks
1 tablespoon lemon juice
salt and pepper, to taste
MUSHROOM & DILL BUTTER:
155 g (5 oz) mushrooms (see note)
90 g (3 oz) unsalted butter
½ teaspoon grated lemon rind
2 tablespoons chopped dill
TO GARNISH:
mange tout (snow peas), blanched
sprigs of dill

Preheat oven to 190C (375F/Gas 5).

Place each salmon steak on a square of foil, sprinkle with lemon juice, salt and pepper. Wrap foil to enclose salmon and put on a baking sheet. Bake in the oven for 15-20 minutes, until fish is cooked.

Meanwhile, prepare mushroom and dill butter. Leave a few mushrooms whole for garnish; finely chop the rest. In a small saucepan, melt 30 g (1 oz) butter and sauté whole mushrooms for 1 minute, until just tender. Remove from the pan and set aside. Add chopped mushrooms to pan and cook for 2-3 minutes, to soften. Transfer to a small bowl and let stand for 1-2 minutes to cool a little. Stir in lemon rind, dill and remaining butter.

Remove skin and central bone from salmon. Transfer to warmed serving plates and top with mushroom and dill butter. Garnish with mange tout (snow peas), reserved whole mushrooms and dill. Serve immediately.

Serves 4.

Note: Fairy rings and tiny button mushrooms, because of their small size, are prettiest for this dish. Alternatively, use a mixture of wild or cultivated mushrooms and, if they are large, slice the few for garnish.

Spiced Roast Chicken

1.75 kg (3½ lb) roasting chicken
15 g (½ oz) butter
155 ml (5 fl oz/⅔ cup) marsala
STUFFING:
45 g (1½ oz) butter
1 onion, finely chopped
1 teaspoon garam masala
125 g (4 oz) button or chestnut mushrooms, chopped
90 g (3 oz) parsnips, coarsely grated
90 g (3 oz) carrots, coarsely grated
30 g (1 oz) walnuts, crushed
2 teaspoons chopped thyme
60 g (2 oz/1 cup) fresh white breadcrumbs
1 small egg, beaten
salt and pepper, to taste
TO GARNISH:
sprigs of thyme and watercress

Preheat oven to 190C (375F/ Gas 5).

To prepare stuffing, in a large saucepan, melt butter, add onion and sauté for 2 minutes, until softened. Stir in garam masala and cook for 1 minute. Add mushrooms, parsnip and carrot and cook, stirring constantly, for 5 minutes. Remove from heat and stir in walnuts, thyme, breadcrumbs and egg. Season with salt and pepper.

Stuff chicken with mixture and secure the bird with string. Put breast down in a roasting pan with 60 ml (2 fl oz/¼ cup) water and cook in the oven for about 1½ hours. After 45 minutes, turn the chicken breast side up and dot with butter. Continue cooking until the skin is golden and the bird is cooked. Transfer to a plate and keep warm.

Pour off any fat from the roasting pan, then add the marsala to the remaining cooking juices, scraping up any sediment. Cook over high heat for 1 minute to reduce slightly. Check seasoning.

Carve chicken and garnish with thyme and watercress. Serve with the stuffing, flavoured meat juices and seasonal vegetables.

Serves 4.

Chicken in Black Bean Sauce

375 g (12 oz) chicken breast, cut into strips

4 teaspoons sesame oil

4 teaspoons corn or groundnut oil

4 spring onions, sliced diagonally

185 g (6 oz) fresh shiitake mushrooms, sliced (see note)

250 g (8 oz) broccoli flowerets

4 tablespoons preserved black beans, rinsed

155 ml (5 fl oz/⅔ cup) chicken stock

2 teaspoons cornflour, blended with a little water

MARINADE:

155 ml (5 fl oz/⅔ cup) dry sherry

2 tablespoons soy sauce

1 teaspoon light soft brown sugar

1 clove garlic, crushed

2.5 cm (1 in) fresh root (green) ginger, grated

1 red chilli, seeded and thinly sliced

Put all marinade ingredients in a shallow bowl and mix well. Add chicken and leave to marinate for at least 1 hour. Remove with a slotted spoon, reserving marinade.

In a wok or large frying pan, heat sesame and corn or groundnut oils, add chicken and stir-fry over high heat for 4 minutes, to seal and brown. Add spring onions, mushrooms, broccoli and black beans and stir-fry for 4 minutes.

Make reserved marinade up to 315 ml (10 fl oz/1¼ cups) with stock and mix with blended cornflour. Pour into the wok or pan and cook, stirring constantly, until sauce is thickened.

Serve immediately, with plain boiled rice or thin egg noodles.

Serves 4.

Note: If fresh shiitake are unavailable, substitute button or small cup mushrooms. Alternatively, use 6 dried shiitake, reconstituted first in warm water for 20 minutes.

Duck with Raspberry Sauce

4 boneless duck breasts
3 teaspoons clear honey
1 clove garlic, crushed
125 ml (4 fl oz/½ cup) Madeira or sweet sherry
30 g (1 oz) butter
4 large flat mushrooms
125 g (4 oz) raspberries
3 tablespoons double (thick) cream
salt and pepper, to taste
TO GARNISH:
sprigs of chervil or coriander

Using a fork, prick the skin of each duck breast several times. Spread with honey and garlic and put in a bowl. Pour over Madeira or sherry and leave to marinate for at least 1 hour.

Remove duck with a slotted spoon, reserving marinade. In a large frying pan, melt butter, add duck and cook over high heat for 2 minutes, turning once, to brown; lower the heat and cook for 10-12 minutes, until the flesh is just pink and the skin a deep, rich brown. Transfer to a plate and keep warm.

Increase heat and add mushrooms to pan, turning quickly in the duck juices. Pour in reserved marinade and cook for 1 minute; transfer mushrooms to plate and keep warm.

Add raspberries to pan and cook over high heat to reduce the liquid until slightly syrupy. Remove from heat, stir in cream and season with salt and pepper.

To serve, slice each duck breast and arrange on warmed serving plates with the mushrooms. Spoon sauce over and around mushrooms. Garnish with chervil or coriander.

Serves 4.

Lamb & Mushroom Blanquette

60 g (2 oz) butter

750 g (1½ lb) lean shoulder of lamb, cut into 3.5 cm (1½ in) pieces

625 ml (20 fl oz/2½ cups) lamb stock

125 ml (4 oz/½ cup) dry white wine

1 onion, quartered

½ teaspoon saffron strands

2 egg yolks

155 ml (5 fl oz/⅔ cup) whipping cream

2 teaspoons lemon juice

salt and white pepper, to taste

1 clove garlic, halved

185 g (6 oz) wild mushrooms (see note)

TO GARNISH:

small bundles of spring vegetables, lightly cooked

In a large saucepan, melt half the butter, add lamb and sauté for 2 minutes, to seal; do not allow to brown. Pour in stock and wine, bring to the boil, then skim the surface. Add onion and saffron, cover and simmer for 1½-2 hours, until lamb is tender, skimming surface occasionally.

Using a fine sieve, strain stock; discard onion and set aside lamb; keep warm. Return stock to the pan and, over a high heat, reduce to half its original volume. Lower heat to a gentle simmer. Mix egg yolks and cream together and whisk into the stock; heat gently but do not allow to boil. Season with lemon juice, salt and white pepper.

In a small frying pan, melt remaining butter, add garlic and mushrooms and sauté for 2-3 minutes, until mushrooms are tender; discard garlic.

To serve, arrange lamb on a warmed serving platter or individual plates. Spoon the sauce over to coat. Arrange mushrooms alongside meat and garnish with bundles of spring vegetables.

Serves 4.

Note: Use a mixture of whatever wild mushrooms are available; fairy rings, morels, oysters, and chanterelles make a pretty, flavoursome garnish. Alternatively use a combination of cultivated varieties.

Beef Casseroled in Stout

60 g (2 oz) butter
60 ml (2 fl oz/¼ cup) olive oil
750 g (1½ lb) topside or chuck steak, cut into 2.5 cm (1 in) dice
30 g (1 oz) plain flour
315 ml (10 fl oz/1¼ cups) stout
2 cloves garlic, halved
3 teaspoons chopped rosemary
12 baby onions
155 g (5 oz) baby carrots
beef stock or water (optional)
185 g (6 oz) button mushrooms
salt and pepper, to taste
TO GARNISH:
sprigs of rosemary

Preheat oven to 160C (325F/Gas 3).

In a large saucepan, heat half the butter and oil. Add meat, in batches if necessary, and cook over high heat to seal. Transfer to a casserole.

Add remaining oil to pan, stir in flour and cook for 2 minutes. Remove from heat and gradually stir in stout. Heat gently, stirring, to form a smooth sauce. Add to casserole with garlic and rosemary. Cover and cook in the oven for 2½ hours, stirring occasionally.

One hour before the end of cooking time, melt remaining butter in a small frying pan, add baby onions and sauté for 2-3 minutes, to brown. Stir into casserole with carrots. Check the quantity of liquid, adding a little stock or water if needed to cover the meat. Return to the oven.

Half an hour before the end of the cooking time, stir in mushrooms. Season with salt and pepper.

Serve, garnished with rosemary and accompanied by new potatoes or rice and crusty bread.

Serves 4.

Filets de Boeuf en Croûtes

60 g (2 oz) butter

4 fillet steaks, each about 2.5 cm (1 in)
thick

185 g (6 oz) fresh wild mushrooms
(see note)

2 tablespoons brandy

375 g (12 oz) puff pastry

185 g (6 oz) goose liver pâté with
truffles (see note)

salt and pepper, to taste

1 egg, beaten

Preheat oven to 230C (450F/Gas 8).

In a large frying pan, melt butter, add fillet steaks and cook for 1 minute on each side, to seal. Transfer to a plate and leave to cool.

Add mushrooms to pan and sauté for 1 minute. Pour in brandy and scrape up the sediments in the pan. Ignite to burn off the alcohol. Set aside.

On a lightly floured surface, roll out pastry to a 30.5 cm (12 in) square; cut into 4 squares. Divide pâté between the squares, piling in the centre. Cover pâté with mushrooms and their cooking juices and place steaks on top. Season with salt and pepper.

Brush pastry edges with water and draw up the corners together to form small parcels. Crimp the edges to seal and turn parcels over, seam side down. Using a sharp knife, mark the top of each parcel with a lattice pattern, taking care not to cut right through. Put on a baking sheet and glaze with beaten egg. Cook in the oven for 25-30 minutes, until pastry is well risen and golden brown.

Serve with new potatoes and a green vegetable, such as asparagus.

Serves 4.

Note: Use parasols, chanterelles, horse mushrooms, ceps or other boletus for this recipe.

Goose liver pâté with truffles is available in cans or jars from specialist shops and good delicatessens. Other pâtés can be substituted.

Pork with Oyster Mushrooms

500 g (1 lb) pork tenderloin
220 g (7 oz/3⅔ cups) white breadcrumbs, from day-old bread
grated rind of ½ lemon
salt and pepper, to taste
1 egg, beaten with 2 tablespoons water
60 g (2 oz) butter
185 g (6 oz) oyster mushrooms, quartered if large
1 clove garlic, crushed
60 ml (2 fl oz/¼ cup) Madeira
155 ml (5 fl oz/⅔ cup) double (thick) cream
TO GARNISH:
lemon slices
sprigs of parsley

Cut pork tenderloin, diagonally, into 1 cm (½ in) slices; beat with a rolling pin to flatten. Mix together breadcrumbs, lemon rind, and salt and pepper. Dip pork pieces into beaten egg, then into seasoned breadcrumbs to coat completely.

In a large frying pan, melt 45 g (1½ oz) butter and sauté the pork for 2 minutes on each side, until tender; do this in batches, if necessary. Transfer to a warmed dish and keep warm. Wipe out pan with absorbent kitchen paper.

Melt remaining butter in the same pan, add mushrooms and garlic and sauté for 1 minute or until tender. Remove mushrooms from pan; keep warm. Add Madeira to pan and cook over high heat until liquid is reduced by half, then lower heat and stir in cream. Season with salt and pepper.

Arrange the pork and mushrooms on warmed serving plates. Spoon the sauce over the mushrooms and garnish with lemon slices and parsley. Serve with green vegetables or a crisp salad.

Serves 4.

Pork Tenderloin with Truffles

125 g (4 oz) fresh horn of plenty mushrooms, or 22 g (¾ oz) dried
2 pork tenderloins, 375 g (12 oz) each
2 cloves garlic, cut into slivers
15 g (½ oz) black truffles, cut into slivers
60 g (2 oz) butter
salt and pepper, to taste
250 ml (8 fl oz/1 cup) dry white wine
BEURRE MANIÉ:
15 g (½ oz) butter
1 teaspoon plain flour
TO GARNISH:
sprigs of thyme or chervil

Preheat oven to 190C (375F/Gas 5). If using dried mushrooms, put in a small bowl, cover with warm water and soak for 20 minutes; rinse, drain well and set aside.

Trim each pork tenderloin to the same length and slit both lengthwise down the centre, taking care not to cut right through. Lay out flat and make 2 more cuts lengthwise down each piece to flatten meat further.

Put garlic slivers along one fillet; cover with mushrooms and truffles. Dot with half the butter and sprinkle with pepper. Cover with the other tenderloin and tie securely with string at 2.5 cm (1 in) intervals.

In a large frying pan, melt remaining butter and brown pork on all sides. Transfer to a small roasting pan with the cooking juices. Pour in wine and cook in the oven for 20-30 minutes or until juices run clear. Transfer meat to a plate and keep warm; reserve cooking juices.

Knead butter and flour together to make *beurre manié*.

Cook the meat juices over high heat for 1 minute to reduce slightly. Add *beurre manié*, stirring constantly, to thicken. Season with salt and pepper.

Serve the tenderloin in slices with sauce spooned around and garnished with thyme or chervil.

Serves 4.

Note: Horn of plenty are used here to extend the much rarer black truffle. The black mushrooms disguise the use of a tiny quantity of truffle well.

Ham & Mushroom Pasta

22 g (¾ oz) dried ceps (porcini)
30 g (1 oz) butter
1 shallot, finely chopped
60 g (2 oz) button mushrooms, quartered
185 g (6 oz) dolcelatte cheese, cubed
155 ml (5 fl oz/⅔ cup) double (thick) cream
45 g (1½ oz) proscuitto ham, cut into strips
pepper, to taste
500 g (1 lb) fresh tagliatelle
TO SERVE:
green salad
cherry tomatoes

Put dried ceps in a small bowl, add warm water to cover and leave to soak for 20 minutes; rinse, drain well and roughly chop.

In a saucepan, melt butter, add shallot and sauté for 2 minutes, to soften. Add ceps and button mushrooms and sauté for 3 minutes, until button mushrooms are just beginning to brown. Stir in dolcelatte, cream and proscuitto and heat gently, stirring constantly, until hot and well blended; season with pepper.

Cook tagliatelle in boiling salted water for about 3 minutes, until *al dente*; drain thoroughly.

Add tagliatelle to the sauce and toss well. Serve accompanied by a green salad and cherry tomatoes.

Serves 4.

Variation: Substitute cream cheese with garlic and herbs or plain cream cheese for the dolcelatte if a milder flavoured sauce is preferred.

Risotto con Funghi

30 g (1 oz) dried ceps (porcini)
125 g (4 oz) butter
1 small onion, finely chopped
375 g (12 oz/2 cups) risotto rice
125 g (4 oz) fresh mushrooms, quartered or sliced (see note)
155 ml (5 fl oz/⅔ cup) dry white wine
1.25 litres (40 fl oz/5 cups) hot chicken stock
3 tablespoons freshly grated Parmesan cheese
salt and pepper, to taste
TO GARNISH:
chopped parsley
sprigs of parsley

Put dried ceps in a small bowl, cover with warm water and leave to soak for 20 minutes; rinse, drain well and roughly chop.

In a saucepan, melt half the butter, add onion and sauté for 4-5 minutes, until golden. Stir in rice and fresh mushrooms and cook for 2-3 minutes, until rice is translucent. Add wine and ceps and cook for about 3 minutes, until wine is absorbed. Lower the heat, add half the chicken stock, cover and simmer for about 10 minutes or until almost all the stock is absorbed.

Add a further 315 ml (10 fl oz/1¼ cups) stock to the pan and continue cooking as before. At this stage keep checking and adding a little stock as necessary until rice is cooked and all liquid absorbed. The total cooking time will depend on the variety of rice (20-30 minutes). Stir in remaining butter and Parmesan and season with salt and pepper.

Transfer to warmed serving plates and sprinkle with chopped parsley. Garnish with sprigs of parsley and serve with a tomato salad.

Serves 4-6.

Note: The flavour of dried ceps is incomparable, but for visual appeal and texture I like to add fresh mushrooms to this dish. Use fresh ceps, sliced, if you can or button mushrooms, cut into quarters. Avoid flat mushrooms, for although the flavour is good, they tend to colour the risotto grey.

Stuffed Mushrooms

90 g (3 oz) shelled Brazil nuts
1 teaspoon olive oil
½ teaspoon salt
8 large flat mushrooms (see note)
60 g (2 oz) butter
2 onions, chopped
1 clove garlic, crushed
3 teaspoons chopped thyme
60 g (2 oz) fresh breadcrumbs
grated rind and juice of 1 lemon
60 g (2 oz/½ cup) grated matured
Cheddar or gruyère cheese
salt and pepper, to taste
TO GARNISH:
sprigs of thyme
lemon slices

Preheat grill to medium high. Mix together Brazil nuts, oil and salt. Put on a baking sheet and toast under the grill for about 3 minutes, stirring frequently, until browned. Leave to cool, then chop very finely and set aside.

Remove stalks from mushrooms; chop stalks and set aside.

In a large frying pan, melt butter and use half to brush mushroom caps. Put stem side down on a baking sheet.

Reheat remaining butter, add onions and garlic to pan and cook for 5 minutes, until onions are softened and golden brown. Add thyme and chopped mushroom stalks and cook for 1 minute. Transfer to a bowl and stir in Brazil nuts and remaining ingredients, mixing well; set aside.

Cook buttered mushroom caps under the grill for 3 minutes, turning once. Divide Brazil nut and lemon stuffing between the mushrooms and grill for 4-6 minutes, until the stuffing is very hot.

Serve immediately, garnished with thyme and lemon slices. Accompany with a green salad.

Serves 4.

Note: Freshly picked wild field mushrooms are preferable to the cultivated flat mushrooms to be found in the shops.

Mushroom & Herb Roulade

185 g (6 oz) mushrooms, finely chopped (see note)
1 bay leaf
315 ml (10 fl oz/1¼ cups) milk
60 g (2 oz) butter
60 g (2 oz/½ cup) plain flour
60 g (2 oz/½ cup) grated Emmental cheese
½ teaspoon Dijon mustard
4 eggs, separated
1 hard-boiled egg, sieved yolk only
2 tablespoons finely chopped herbs (chives, dill or parsley)
2 tablespoons double (thick) cream
salt and pepper, to taste
sprigs of herbs, to garnish

Preheat oven to 200C (400F/Gas 6). Grease and line a 23 x 33 cm (9 x 13 in) Swiss roll tin with non-stick paper.

Put mushrooms, bay leaf and half the milk in a saucepan, bring to the boil, then simmer for 2 minutes. Remove from heat, cover and leave for 10-15 minutes. Strain, reserving mushrooms and liquid; discard bay leaf. Add remaining milk to liquid.

In the same pan, melt butter, stir in flour and cook for 1 minute.

Remove from the heat and gradually stir in milk. Cook, stirring, to form a smooth thick sauce. Stir in cheese and mustard. Transfer one third to a bowl and keep warm.

To the sauce remaining in the pan add reserved mushrooms and egg yolks, one at a time, stirring well. In a bowl, whisk egg whites until stiff, then fold into mushroom mixture. Pour into prepared tin and bake in the oven for 12-15 minutes, until golden and firm.

Meanwhile, to reserved sauce, add sieved egg yolk and herbs. Stir in cream and seasoning.

Turn the roulade onto greaseproof paper and peel away lining paper. Spread with the reserved sauce, then roll up, from a short side.

Serve immediately, in slices, garnished with herbs and accompanied by a green salad.

Serves 4.

Note: Use parasols or horse mushrooms if you can get them; if not, use cultivated varieties.

Hot Mushroom Soufflé

60 g (2 oz) butter
250 g (8 oz) mushrooms, chopped (see note)
60 g (2 oz/½ cup) plain flour
315 ml (10 fl oz/1¼ cups) milk
90 g (3 oz/¾ cup) grated Emmental cheese
salt and pepper, to taste
3 eggs, separated
TO GARNISH:
sprigs of parsley

Preheat oven to 220C (425F/Gas 7). Grease a deep 1 litre (32 fl oz/4 cup) soufflé dish.

In a saucepan, melt butter, add mushrooms and sauté for about 5 minutes, until tender; if they exude a lot of liquid, remove with a slotted spoon and cook the juices over high heat until reduced before returning mushrooms to pan.

Add flour and cook, stirring, constantly, for 2 minutes. Remove pan from the heat and gradually stir in milk. Return to the heat and cook, stirring, until smooth and very thick; stir in cheese. Remove from the heat and season with salt and pepper. Leave to cool slightly, then beat in egg yolks, one at a time.

In a bowl, whisk egg whites until stiff, then carefully fold into mushroom mixture. Pour into prepared soufflé dish and bake in the centre of the oven for 40-45 minutes, until well risen and browned. Serve immediately, garnished with parsley.

Serves 4.

Note: Horn of plenty, chanterelles, horse mushrooms and the aniseed flavoured wood mushrooms are particularly suitable for this recipe.

Baked Stuffed Avocados

15 g (½ oz) butter
250 g (8 oz) mushrooms, chopped (see note)
4 teaspoons plain flour
pinch of dry mustard
155 ml (5 fl oz/⅔ cup) milk
60 g (2 oz/½ cup) grated matured Cheddar cheese
salt and pepper, to taste
4 small ripe avocados
1 egg, separated
HERBED CRUMBS:
30 g (1 oz) butter
60 g (2 oz) fresh white breadcrumbs
pinch of celery salt
2 teaspoons chopped dill
2 teaspoons chopped parsley
TO GARNISH:
salad leaves

Preheat oven to 200C (400F/Gas 6). First, prepare herbed crumbs: in a small saucepan, melt butter, add breadcrumbs and cook for 3-4 minutes, stirring constantly, until just beginning to colour. Remove from the heat and stir in celery salt, dill and parsley; set aside.

In a separate saucepan, melt butter, add mushrooms and sauté for 3 minutes to soften. Stir in flour and mustard and cook for 1 minute. Remove from heat and gradually stir in milk; cook, stirring constantly, to form a smooth thick sauce. Stir in cheese. Remove from heat and season with salt and pepper.

Cut avocados in half and discard the stones. Scoop out some of the flesh, leaving a 1 cm (½ in) border. Roughly chop flesh and add to the sauce. Stir in egg yolk.

In a bowl, whisk egg white until stiff, then fold into the sauce. Divide between the avocado shells and put on a baking sheet. Sprinkle with the herbed crumbs and bake in the oven for about 25 minutes, until hot. Serve immediately, garnished with salad leaves.

Serves 4.

Note: Parasols, chanterelles, hedgehog fungus or shaggy ink caps are ideal for this recipe. Otherwise try cultivated chestnut mushrooms in preference to button varieties.

Brie & Mushroom Flan

PASTRY:

250 g (8 oz/2 cups) plain flour

pinch of salt

125 g (4 oz) butter or margarine

FILLING:

30 g (1 oz) butter

185 g (6 oz) mushrooms, sliced (see note)

250 g (8 oz) spinach leaves, shredded

315 g (10 oz) brie, rind removed, diced

3 eggs

155 ml (5 fl oz/⅔ cup) single (light) cream

salt and pepper, to taste

Preheat oven to 200C (400F/Gas 6).

To make pastry, sift flour and salt into a large bowl and rub in butter or margarine until the mixture resembles breadcrumbs. Add about 3 tablespoons water and mix to a firm dough.

On a lightly floured surface, roll out pastry and use to line an oiled 20 cm (8 in) flan tin. Prick the base and chill for 15 minutes, then bake blind in the oven for 10-12 minutes. Lower temperature to 180C (350F/Gas 4).

Meanwhile, prepare filling. In a large frying pan, melt butter, add mushrooms and sauté for 1-2 minutes. Add spinach and cook for 1-2 minutes, until wilted. Strain in a sieve, pressing out excess liquid, then transfer to pastry case. Tuck brie cubes into spinach and mushroom mixture. Beat together eggs and cream, season with salt and pepper and pour over spinach mixture. Bake in the oven for 30-35 minutes or until the filling is set.

Serve warm for preference, or cold, with salad.

Serves 6.

Note: Use cultivated button mushrooms or wild varieties if they are available, such as chanterelles, horse mushrooms and parasols, or a mixture of these.

Spinach & Feta Parcel

60 g (2 oz) butter

1 shallot, finely chopped

1 clove garlic, crushed

375 g (12 oz) mushrooms, finely chopped (see note)

90 ml (3 fl oz/⅓ cup) white wine

4 teaspoons tomato purée (paste)

1 tablespoon chopped dill

salt and pepper, to taste

250 g (8 oz) spinach, chopped

250 g (8 oz) feta cheese, crumbled

1 egg yolk

pinch of freshly grated nutmeg

8 sheets of filo pastry

Preheat oven to 200C (400F/Gas 6). In a saucepan, melt half the butter, add shallot and garlic and sauté for 2 minutes. Add mushrooms, wine and tomato purée (paste) and cook over high heat, stirring frequently, for 8-10 minutes or until all the liquid has evaporated. Stir in dill, season with salt and pepper and set aside.

Cook spinach, with just the water clinging to the leaves after washing, for 2-3 minutes, until wilted. Drain thoroughly, squeezing out excess water, and transfer to a bowl. Add cheese and egg yolk, season with nutmeg and mix well.

Melt remaining butter. Brush a baking sheet with butter and put a single sheet of filo pastry on the base. Brush lightly with butter, cover with a second sheet of pastry and brush again. Spread the mushroom mixture over the pastry, leaving a 2.5 cm (1 in) border, and cover with the spinach mixture. Dampen the pastry edges and cover with a filo sheet; brush with butter. Continue to layer remaining pastry, brushing each sheet with butter. Seal edges and, with a sharp knife, score a deep cross on the surface. Bake in the oven for about 25 minutes, until pastry is crisp and golden brown.

Serve hot or warm, quartered or in slices, with salad and new potatoes.

Serves 4.

Note: Use field or horse mushrooms or parasols or, if unavailable, the cultivated open cup variety.

Scrambled Egg with Truffles

6 eggs

15 g (½ oz) fresh or canned white truffles

salt and pepper, to taste

6-8 asparagus spears

2 slices wholewheat bread

45 g (1 ½ oz) butter

2 tablespoons double (thick) cream

TO GARNISH:

sprigs of chervil

In a bowl, beat eggs. Cut truffles into very fine slivers; set half aside. Add the rest to the eggs; if using canned truffles add any juices as well. Season with salt and pepper, cover and leave to stand for at least 2 hours.

When almost ready to cook eggs, prepare asparagus. Break off the woody stalk ends and, using a potato peeler, thinly peel the stems. Cook in boiling water for about 5 minutes, until just tender; drain and keep hot.

Meanwhile, toast bread and spread with half the butter; keep hot.

In a non-stick saucepan, melt remaining butter over low heat. Add egg and truffle mixture and cook, stirring lightly with a wooden spoon, for about 3 minutes, until eggs begin to thicken and set; take care not to overcook – the eggs should be creamy and soft. Stir in cream.

Arrange asparagus and hot toast on 2 warmed serving plates and divide scrambled egg between them. Sprinkle with reserved truffle. Garnish with chervil and serve immediately.

Serves 2.

Omelette with Chanterelles

5 eggs

2 tablespoons chopped herbs, e.g.
parsley, chervil, chives, tarragon, dill

30 g (1 oz) butter

FILLING:

15 g (½ oz) butter

1 clove garlic, halved

250 g (8 oz) chanterelles

2 tablespoons double (thick) cream

salt and pepper, to taste

TO GARNISH:

sprigs of herbs

First prepare filling: in a small frying pan, melt butter, add garlic and cook gently for 1 minute, taking care not to burn butter; discard garlic. Add chanterelles to the pan and cook over high heat for 5 minutes; if the mushrooms exude a lot of liquid, remove with a slotted spoon and cook the juices until reduced before returning mushrooms to pan.

Remove from the heat, stir in cream and season with salt and pepper. Keep warm while preparing omelette.

In a bowl or jug, beat together eggs, herbs and 3 tablespoons water. In a non-stick frying pan, melt butter, then pour in eggs. Using a spatula, push the edge of the omelette, as it sets, towards the centre, allowing the runny mixture to fill the pan. Continue cooking in this way until the omelette is almost set.

Spoon the filling over half the omelette, then fold over the other half to enclose. Cut in half and slide onto warmed serving plates. Garnish with herbs and serve immediately.

Serves 2.

Note: Eggs for omelettes are exquisite when scented by truffles. Simply store a truffle with the eggs.

Tagliatelle with Mushrooms

15 g (½ oz) dried ceps (porcini)
30 g (1 oz) butter
250 g (8 oz) small button mushrooms, quartered
1 clove garlic, crushed
155 ml (5 fl oz/⅔ cup) dry white wine
2 eggs
125 ml (4 fl oz/½ cup) double (thick) cream
500 g (1 lb) fresh tagliatelle
3-4 tablespoons freshly grated Parmesan cheese
salt and pepper, to taste
1 tablespoon chopped parsley
TO GARNISH:
sprigs of parsley

Soak dried ceps in warm water for 20 minutes. Rinse well to remove any grit, then chop.

In a saucepan, melt butter, add button mushrooms and garlic and sauté for 2 minutes. Add ceps and wine and cook over high heat for 2-3 minutes, until mushrooms are tender and liquid has been reduced by half; keep hot.

Beat together eggs and cream.

Cook tagliatelle in plenty of boiling salted water for about 3 minutes, until *al dente*; drain well and return to pan. Add eggs and mushroom mixture to pasta and toss until eggs become creamy and begin to set. Add Parmesan, salt and pepper and toss again. Serve immediately, sprinkled with chopped parsley and garnished with parsley sprigs.

Serves 4.

Note: If you are fortunate enough to find fresh ceps or other boletus, use these to replace both dried ceps and button mushrooms. You will need about 250 g (8 oz), chopped.

Pasta, Beans & Mushrooms

250 g (8 oz) dried rigatoni
salt
500 g (1 lb) broad beans in their pods, shelled
30 g (1 oz) butter, or 2 tablespoons virgin olive oil
SAUCE:
2 tablespoons virgin olive oil
2 shallots, finely chopped
1 clove garlic, crushed
2-3 tablespoons chopped sun-dried tomato (see note, page 75)
375 g (12 oz) wild mushrooms, chopped if large (see note)
2 tablespoons finely chopped parsley
250 ml (8 fl oz/1 cup) passata
4 tablespoons double (thick) cream
salt and pepper, to taste
TO SERVE·
freshly grated Parmesan cheese
sprigs of parsley

First, prepare sauce: in a saucepan, heat oil, add shallot and garlic and sauté for 3-4 minutes, until softened and just beginning to colour. Stir in tomato, mushrooms and parsley and cook for 2 minutes, stirring constantly. Stir in passata and simmer for 5-6 minutes, until mushrooms are tender. Stir in cream and heat gently. Season with salt and pepper and set aside.

Cook rigatoni in plenty of boiling salted water for 8-10 minutes, until *al dente*. In a separate pan, cook broad beans in boiling water for 5-6 minutes until tender. Drain pasta and beans thoroughly and put in a large warmed serving bowl. Toss together with butter or oil and a little more salt if desired.

Gently reheat sauce; do not boil. Add half to bowl and toss lightly to mix. Serve rigatoni and beans on warmed plates with remaining sauce spooned over. Sprinkle with Parmesan and garnish with parsley.

Serves 4.

Note: Use field or parasol mushrooms, morels, or ceps and other large boletus.

Mushroom Stroganoff

30 g (1 oz) butter

2 tablespoons virgin olive oil

2 onions, thinly sliced

1-2 cloves garlic, crushed

750 g (1½ lb) ceps or large field mushrooms, sliced

4 tablespoons brandy

315 ml (10 fl oz/1¼ cups) thick sour cream

salt and pepper, to taste

TO GARNISH:

paprika

few chives

In a large frying pan, heat butter and oil, add onions and cook for 3-4 minutes, until softened and beginning to colour. Add garlic and mushrooms and cook for 2 minutes, stirring constantly.

Stir in brandy and cook for 3-4 minutes, stirring frequently, until mushrooms are tender. Lower the heat and stir in thick sour cream; heat gently, taking care not to boil. Season with salt and pepper.

Sprinkle with paprika and garnish with chives. Serve with saffron rice or warm crusty bread.

Serves 4.

Note: Large 'meaty' textured mushrooms are essential for this dish: ceps or other boletus, or field mushrooms, are best. For appearance as well as flavour choose ceps, as field mushrooms will colour the sauce grey. Cultivated flat mushrooms lack flavour but can be used, with good results, with the help of dried mushrooms such as porcini or suillus.

Mushroom & Broccoli Stir-Fry

125 g (4 oz) firm tofu, cut into 2 cm (¾ in) cubes

2 tablespoons soy sauce

4 dried shiitake mushrooms

2-3 tablespoons groundnut or olive oil

250 g (8 oz) broccoli flowerets

1 clove garlic, crushed

2 teaspoons shredded fresh root (green) ginger

1 red onion, cut into thin wedges

125 g (4 oz) canned straw mushrooms, drained

3 tablespoons dry sherry

1 teaspoon cornflour

good pinch of sugar

black or Szechuan pepper, to taste

1 teaspoon sesame seeds, toasted

TO GARNISH:

sprigs of coriander

In a small bowl, toss tofu in soy sauce and leave to marinate until required.

Put shiitake in a small bowl, add 125 ml (4 fl oz/½ cup) hot water and leave to soak for 20 minutes. When reconstituted, add soaking liquor to tofu mixture. Slice mushroom caps, discarding stalks.

In a wok, heat oil. Using a slot-ted spoon remove tofu from marinade, reserving marinade, add to wok and stir-fry over high heat for 1 minute, until browned; remove and set aside.

Add broccoli, garlic and ginger to wok and stir-fry for 2 minutes. Add onion, shiitake and straw mush-rooms and stir-fry for 1 minute. Pour in tofu marinade and bring to the boil, then simmer for 2 minutes. Stir in tofu.

Blend together sherry, cornflour and sugar, then pour into wok and cook, stirring until thickened. Season with pepper and transfer to a warmed serving dish.

Sprinkle with toasted sesame seeds and garnish with coriander. Serve immediately, accompanied by hot rice or noodles.

Serves 4.

Note: Dried wood ear mushrooms may also be added, for their pretty, frilly appearance and crisp texture, rather than flavour. Reconstitute them with the shiitake.

Wild Rice Salad

185 g (6 oz) wholewheat, soaked overnight

45 g (1½ oz) wild rice

125 g (4 oz) gruyère cheese, diced

125 g (4 oz) Pipo Crème, or other creamy blue cheese, diced

10 cherry tomatoes, halved

2 spring onions, shredded

4 tablespoons virgin olive oil

250 g (8 oz) mixed chanterelles and oyster mushrooms

1 clove garlic, chopped

2 tablespoons wine vinegar

2 tablespoons chopped dill

pinch of sugar (optional)

salt and pepper, to taste

TO GARNISH:

sprigs of dill

In a large saucepan, cook wholewheat and wild rice together in boiling water for 20 minutes, until just tender. Rinse under running cold water, drain thoroughly and leave to cool. Transfer to a large salad bowl and add cheeses, tomatoes and spring onions.

In a large frying pan, heat oil, add mushrooms and sauté for 4 minutes. Remove from the heat and add garlic, vinegar, dill and sugar, if desired; season with salt and pepper. Add to the salad and toss lightly to mix. Serve, immediately or after chilling, garnished with dill.

Serves 4-6.

Saffron Rice Pilaff

generous pinch of saffron strands
1 tablespoon sesame or olive oil
60 g (2 oz/½ cup) slivered almonds
45 g (1½ oz) butter
1 onion, chopped
1 clove garlic, crushed
1 large carrot, cut into matchstick pieces
1 stick celery, cut into matchstick pieces
250 g (8 oz/1½ cups) brown rice
315 g (10 oz) mixed chanterelles and oyster mushrooms
60 g (2 oz/⅓ cup) sultanas
625 ml (20 fl oz/2½ cups) mushroom or vegetable stock
125 g (4 oz) mange tout (snow peas), halved
1-2 tablespoons chopped coriander
salt and pepper, to taste
TO GARNISH:
coriander leaves
marigold petals (optional)

In a small bowl or cup, soak saffron strands in 4 tablespoons boiling water for 20 minutes.

In a saucepan, heat oil, add almonds and cook, stirring constantly for 1-2 minutes, to brown. Transfer to a plate and set aside.

Add butter to pan and heat gently, until melted. Add onion, garlic, carrot and celery and cook for 3-4 minutes, until just softened. Add rice and cook for 4 minutes, stirring occasionally. Stir in mushrooms, sultanas, saffron with its soaking liquid and stock and bring to the boil. Lower the heat, cover and cook for 25-30 minutes, until rice is tender.

Two minutes before the end of cooking time stir in mange tout (snow peas), coriander and reserved almonds. Season with salt and pepper.

Garnish the pilaff with coriander leaves and sprinkle with marigold petals, if desired, to serve.

Serves 4.

Italian Mushroom Salad

1 small head Four Seasons or lollo rosso lettuce
½ red onion, thinly sliced
250 g (8 oz) button mushrooms, thinly sliced
60 g (2 oz) Parmesan cheese
2 teaspoons finely chopped parsley
DRESSING:
5 tablespoons virgin olive oil
finely grated rind of ½ lemon
juice of 1 small lemon
¼ teaspoon wholegrain mustard
pinch of sugar
salt and pepper, to taste

First make dressing: stir all of the ingredients together in a small bowl or put into a screw-top jar and shake well; set aside.

Tear lettuce into bite-sized pieces and arrange on individual serving plates with onion; set aside.

Put mushrooms in a large bowl. Pour over the dressing and toss well to mix. Pare wafer-thin slices of Parmesan and add to mushrooms, tossing lightly to mix.

Arrange on top of the lettuce, sprinkle with parsley and serve immediately.

Serves 4.

Note: The mushrooms may be left to 'marinate' in the dressing for up to 2 hours, but it is best to add the Parmesan to the salad just before serving.

Pepper & Mushroom Salad

1 each green, red and yellow pepper, halved and seeded

2 tablespoons virgin olive oil

1 shallot, finely chopped

1 clove garlic, crushed

185 g (6 oz) wild mushrooms, chopped into large pieces (see note)

1-2 tablespoons red wine vinegar

½ teaspoon Dijon mustard

salt and pepper, to taste

60 g (2 oz) feta cheese, crumbled

TO GARNISH:

sprigs of parsley

To prepare peppers, cook under a hot grill, skin side down, for 3 minutes; turn and cook for 5 minutes or until the skin blisters and blackens. Peel off the skin, cut peppers into 2 cm (¾ in) pieces and arrange on individual serving plates; set aside.

In a frying pan, heat oil, add shallot and garlic and sauté for 2 minutes, to soften. Add mushrooms and cook for 2 minutes. Using a slotted spoon, add the mixture to the peppers.

Add vinegar and mustard to the pan juices and cook over high heat until reduced to 1-2 tablespoons. Season with salt and pepper, then drizzle over the peppers and mushrooms. Leave to cool, then chill for at least 30 minutes. Sprinkle with feta cheese and garnish with parsley to serve.

Serves 4.

Note: A mixture of wild mushrooms is ideal. If unavailable, try a mixture of cultivated oyster mushrooms and sliced cup mushrooms.

Asparagus & Prawn Salad

125 g (4 oz) penne, or other dried pasta
shapes

500 g (1 lb) asparagus

125 g (4 oz) button mushrooms, sliced

185 g (6 oz) peeled prawns, thawed if
frozen

1 spring onion, shredded

125 ml (4 fl oz/½ cup) thick sour
cream

salt and pepper, to taste

TO GARNISH:

lemon slices

few cooked prawns in shell

Cook pasta according to packet instructions, until *al dente*; rinse under running cold water and drain thoroughly. Transfer to a large bowl.

Discard the woody bases from asparagus. Thinly slice half the length of each stalk; cut off tips; set remaining stalk aside. Cook asparagus tips and sliced stalks in boiling water for 1 minute. Refresh in cold water and add to pasta with mushrooms, prawns and spring onion.

Cook remaining asparagus stalks in boiling water for 6-7 minutes or until soft. Transfer to a food processor or blender, add thick sour cream and purée until smooth. Add to pasta salad and toss to mix. Season with salt and pepper.

Transfer to individual serving plates and garnish with lemon slices and prawns.

Serves 2-4.

Mediterranean Lamb Salad

1 small aubergine (eggplant), about 250 g (8 oz), diced
salt
2 tablespoons virgin olive oil
1 small onion, thinly sliced
2 courgettes (zucchini), sliced
185 g (6 oz) wild mushrooms, sliced if large (see note)
4 tomatoes, skinned, seeded and quartered
12 black olives
375 g (12 oz) pink (under done) roast lamb, cut into strips
DRESSING:
3 tablespoons virgin olive oil
2 tablespoons red wine vinegar
2 teaspoons Dijon mustard
1 tablespoon chopped rosemary
1 tablespoon chopped thyme
pinch of sugar
salt and pepper, to taste

First make dressing: mix all ingredients together in a small bowl or put in a screw-top jar and shake; set aside.

Rinse aubergine (eggplant) with cold water and put in a colander. Sprinkle with salt and leave to drain for 20 minutes. Rinse to remove salt and pat dry with a clean tea-towel.

In a large frying pan or wok, heat 1 tablespoon oil, add onion and sauté for 3 minutes. Add aubergine (eggplant) and courgettes (zucchini) and cook for 3-4 minutes, to soften. Transfer to a large salad bowl.

In the same pan, heat remaining oil and sauté mushrooms for 2-3 minutes, until just tender; pour off any excess liquid. Add mushrooms to the salad bowl, with tomatoes, olives and lamb. Pour over prepared dressing and toss well to mix. Chill for at least 20 minutes before serving.

Serves 4-6

Note: Use a mixture of wild mushrooms such as cauliflower fungus, chanterelles, morels, hedgehog fungus and, if you are certain of their identification, any of the russulas.

Cherry Tomato & Bacon Salad

500 g (1 lb) cherry tomatoes

155 g (5 oz) chestnut mushrooms, sliced

2 tablespoons olive oil

6 bacon rashers, rinds removed, diced

1 tablespoon wine vinegar

3 tablespoons thick sour cream

salt and pepper, to taste

TO GARNISH:

4 black olives, chopped

1 tablespoon snipped chives

few chives

Plunge half the tomatoes into a bowl of boiling water for about 30 seconds, then drain and remove skins. Repeat with remainder. Transfer to a salad bowl and add mushrooms.

In a large frying pan, heat oil, add bacon and cook for 2-3 minutes, until crisp; transfer to salad bowl. Deglaze the pan with vinegar, scraping up the sediment, and add to salad with thick sour cream, and salt and pepper. Toss lightly to mix and chill for at least 15 minutes.

Sprinkle with olives and chives and garnish with chives to serve.

Serves 4-6.

Note: I like the earthy flavour of chestnut mushrooms together with bacon in this salad but, if they are not available, use button mushrooms instead.

Salade Tiède

375 g (12 oz) mixed salad leaves (e.g. frisée, mâche, radicchio, red oak leaf, cos, chicory, rocket)
1 red onion, thinly sliced
4 tablespoons hazelnut or virgin olive oil
3 tablespoons pine kernels
4 rashers smoked streaky bacon, rinds removed, diced
1 small clove garlic, crushed
155 g (5 oz) wild mushrooms, sliced (see note)
2 tablespoons raspberry vinegar
pinch of sugar
½ teaspoon Dijon or tarragon mustard
salt and pepper, to taste

Tear salad leaves into bite-sized pieces and put in a salad bowl with the sliced onion.

In a large frying pan, heat 1 tablespoon oil, add pine kernels and cook for 1 minute, stirring constantly, until golden brown; drain on absorbent kitchen paper.

Add bacon to pan and cook for about 3 minutes, until crisp; transfer to a plate.

Heat a further 1 tablespoon oil in the frying pan, add garlic and mushrooms and cook for 3-4 minutes until tender. If the mushrooms exude a lot of liquid, transfer them with a slotted spoon to a plate and reduce the liquid over high heat until only 2 tablespoons remains.

Return bacon and mushrooms, if necessary, to the pan and add remaining oil, vinegar, sugar, mustard and salt and pepper. Heat for a few seconds, stirring, then add to the salad leaves; toss lightly. Sprinkle with prepared pine kernels and serve immediately.

Serves 4.

Note: Use small, pretty mushrooms such as chanterelles, fairy rings, cauliflower fungus or a mixture.

Potato & Mushroom Salad

1 kg (2 lb) waxy salad potatoes (see note)
salt and pepper, to taste
1 small red onion
2 tablespoons virgin olive oil
185 g (6 oz) ceps, roughly chopped
3 teaspoons white wine vinegar
2 tablespoons chopped dill
90 ml (3 fl oz/⅓ cup) double (thick) cream
1 tablespoon wholegrain mustard
TO GARNISH:
sprigs of dill

Cook whole potatoes in boiling salted water for 12-15 minutes, until tender. Drain and leave until cool enough to handle, then thickly slice into a large bowl.

Cut onion into wedges and separate into 'petals'.

In a large frying pan, heat oil, add ceps and onion and sauté for 2 minutes. Add vinegar and cook for 2 minutes, until mushrooms are tender; remove onions and mushrooms with a slotted spoon and add to potatoes.

If the mushrooms have exuded a lot of liquid, reduce over high heat until just 2 tablespoons remains. Add to salad with dill and seasoning, toss lightly to mix and transfer to a serving plate.

Mix together cream and mustard and drizzle over salad. Serve warm or cold, garnished with dill.

Serves 6.

Note: 'Pink Fir Apple' and 'Charlotte' are small waxy potatoes with an elongated shape that is perfect for slicing into salads.

If ceps are not available, you can substitute field or flat mushrooms, although the flavours are not so good.

Orange & Tarragon Mushrooms

3 tablespoons olive oil

1 shallot, finely chopped

500 g (1 lb) small open cup mushrooms

2.5 cm (1 in) piece fresh root (green) ginger, grated

1 clove garlic, crushed

1 tablespoon sesame oil

2 tablespoons balsamic vinegar

1 teaspoon grated orange rind

juice of 1 orange

salt and pepper, to taste

TO SERVE:

2 sticks celery, cut into fine julienne

1 tablespoon chopped tarragon

In a large frying pan, heat 2 tablespoons olive oil, add shallot and sauté for 3-4 minutes, until lightly browned. Add mushrooms, ginger and garlic and cook for 4-5 minutes, stirring frequently, until mushrooms are tender. Using a slotted spoon, transfer vegetables to a bowl.

To the juices in the pan, add remaining ingredients and cook over high heat until the liquid has reduced by half. Pour over the mushrooms and leave to cool, then chill for at least 30 minutes.

To serve, arrange mushrooms on a serving plate, surround with celery julienne and sprinkle with tarragon.

Serves 4.

Scented Garlic Mushrooms

375 g (12 oz) button mushrooms
155 ml (5 fl oz/²⁄₃ cup) white wine
1 bay leaf
seeds of 2 white cardamom pods
2 cloves garlic, crushed
3-4 tablespoons thick sour cream
salt and pepper, to taste
TO SERVE:
young spinach leaves

Put mushrooms, wine, bay leaf, cardamom seeds and 1 clove garlic in a saucepan. Bring to the boil, then simmer, uncovered, for about 10 minutes, until the mushrooms are tender and the liquid has been reduced by about half.

Leave to cool slightly, then stir in thick sour cream and remaining garlic; discard bay leaf. Season with salt and pepper and chill for at least 30 minutes before serving.

Serve the garlic mushrooms with young spinach leaves.

Serves 4.

Variation: Substitute sliced wood or field blewits, or St Georges mushrooms, for the button mushrooms.

Baked Mushrooms in Madeira

60 g (2 oz) butter

500 g (1 lb) large field mushrooms, thickly sliced

1 large clove garlic, thinly sliced

salt and pepper, to taste

155 ml (5 fl oz/⅔ cup) Madeira

TO GARNISH:

1 tablespoon chopped parsley

Preheat oven to 190C (375F/ Gas 5). Use butter to grease a large flat baking dish. Arrange mushrooms in one layer in the dish and dot evenly with garlic slivers.

Season with salt and pepper and pour over the Madeira.

Bake in the oven for 25-30 minutes, until mushrooms are tender. Serve hot or cold, sprinkled with parsley.

Serves 4.

Note: Cultivated flat mushrooms can be used in this recipe but the flavour will not be as rich as the wild variety. Fresh ceps are delicious cooked in this way.

Mushrooms in Beer Batter

500 g (1 lb) mushrooms (see note)

oil for deep-frying

sea salt

lemon wedges

BATTER:

125 g (4 oz/1 cup) plain flour

½ teaspoon salt

2 eggs, separated

155 ml (5 fl oz/⅔ cup) beer

2 tablespoons sunflower oil

TO GARNISH:

sprigs of chervil

First prepare batter: sift flour and salt into a bowl, add egg yolks, then gradually whisk in beer to form a smooth batter; stir in oil. In a clean bowl, whisk egg whites until soft peaks form, then fold into batter.

Heat oil to 180C (350F). Dip each mushroom into batter and deep-fry, in small batches, in hot oil for 2-3 minutes or until crisp and golden; drain on absorbent kitchen paper.

Serve hot, sprinkled with sea salt and fresh lemon juice and garnished with chervil.

Serves 4.

Note: Choose a mixture of wild and cultivated mushrooms for this accompaniment, aiming for a pretty assortment of shapes. Try small cup mushrooms, oyster mushrooms, morels, shiitake, parasols, chanterelles and small sliced puffballs.

Aubergine (Eggplant) Gâteaux

1 large aubergine (eggplant), thinly sliced

3 tablespoons garlic salt

315 ml (10 fl oz/1¼ cups) passata

3-4 tablespoons virgin olive oil

375 g (12 oz) mushrooms, finely chopped (see note)

1 clove garlic, crushed

1 tablespoon chopped basil

2 tablespoons brandy

salt and pepper, to taste

4 tablespoons crème frâiche or fromage frais

TO GARNISH:

sprigs of parsley and basil

Preheat oven to 180C (350F/ Gas 4). Rinse aubergine (eggplant) and put in a colander. Sprinkle with garlic salt and leave to drain for 20 minutes. Rinse to remove salt and pat dry with a clean tea-towel.

Meanwhile, in a saucepan, boil passata until thickened and reduced by half; set aside.

In a large frying pan, heat 2-3 tablespoons oil and sauté aubergine (eggplant), in batches if necessary, for 1-2 minutes, until just softened.

Use to line 4 ramekins, allowing extra to overlap later.

In the same pan, heat remaining oil, add mushrooms, garlic and basil and cook over high heat for 10-12 minutes, until all the liquid from the mushrooms has evaporated. Add brandy and cook for 2 minutes. Season with salt and pepper and divide between prepared ramekins.

Top with crème frâiche or fromage frais and, finally, with passata. Overlap the aubergine (eggplant) to enclose the filling and press down lightly. Cover each with foil and bake in oven for 20 minutes.

Turn out and garnish with parsley to serve.

Serves 4.

Note: Use field or horse mushrooms or ceps, or a mixture of wild mushrooms, in preference to cultivated varieties.

Serve as a stylish accompaniment to lamb or chicken. The gâteaux may be prepared in advance and baked just before serving.

Creamy Mushroom Potatoes

7 g (¼ oz) dried ceps (porcini) reconstituted and chopped (see note)
125 g (4 oz) button mushrooms, chopped
90 ml (3 fl oz/⅓ cup) single (light) cream
45 g (1½ oz) butter
750 g (1½ lb) potatoes, cut into 3.5 cm (1½ in) dice
salt and pepper, to taste
TO GARNISH:
sprigs of parsley or mixed herbs

Put ceps, mushrooms, cream and butter in a small saucepan and bring to the boil; remove from the heat, cover and leave to infuse for 15 minutes.

Meanwhile, cook potatoes in boiling water for 15 minutes or until soft. Drain well, then return to the pan for a few seconds to dry off. Transfer to a warmed mixing bowl and break up the pieces using a potato masher. Add mushroom mixture and beat with a wooden spoon until smooth and creamy. Season well with salt and pepper.

Transfer to a warmed serving dish and serve immediately, garnished with sprigs of parsley or other herbs.

Serves 4-6.

Note: To reconstitute porcini, put in a small bowl and cover with warm water. Leave to stand for 20 minutes, then rinse to remove any grit. This small amount gives a superb flavour.

If field or flat mushrooms are used instead of button mushrooms the potatoes will be coloured an unappetizing grey.

Potato and Mushroom Cake

60 g (2 oz) butter
750 g (1½ lb) old potatoes, thinly sliced
1 onion, thinly sliced
185 g (6 oz) mushrooms, sliced (see note)
salt and pepper, to taste
freshly grated nutmeg
90 ml (3 fl oz/⅓ cup) double (thick) cream
TO GARNISH:
sprigs of herbs

Preheat oven to 190C (375F/ Gas 5). Line a loose-bottomed 23 cm (9 in) cake tin or flan tin with foil, then grease with a little butter.

Layer potato, onion and mush- room slices in the tin, seasoning layers with salt, pepper and nutmeg and dotting each layer with butter. Finish with a layer of potato.

Pour over cream, cover with foil and bake in the oven for 1 hour. Remove foil and cook for 30 minutes, to crisp the top. Transfer to a warmed serving plate, garnish with herbs and serve hot.

Serves 4-6.

Note: Use chestnut, button or small cup mushrooms. Use ceps, if you are able to obtain them, for their superior flavour; cut into thin, bite- sized pieces.